The Virginia and Federal Rules of Evidence

A Concise Comparison with Commentary

Jeffrey Bellin

William & Mary Law School

Includes Virginia Rule Amendments Effective July 2015

Dedicated to Cathy, Garrett and Zoe

CONTENTS

Jeffrey Bellin

INTRODUCTION

Comparisons of federal and state evidence rules can be immensely helpful to attorneys, judges and law students who are often well versed in one set of rules, but not the other. As a result, book-length federal-to-state rule comparisons exist for most major United States jurisdictions, including California, Florida, New York and Texas. Virginia has until now been a notable exception. This book fills that void.

Virginia replaced its common law of evidence with codified rules in 2012, adding welcome clarity and consistency to litigation in Virginia's courts. The 2012 codification provides a critical foundation for this project. By crystalizing its own evidence rules, Virginia allowed those rules to be contrasted with other codified evidence rules, such as the Federal Rules of Evidence, in a concise volume. Particularly helpful in this respect is the Virginia codifiers' adoption of the same numbering system employed in the federal rules.

The now-codified "Virginia Rules of Evidence" are styled as Part II of the "Rules of the Supreme Court of Virginia." Each Virginia evidence rule begins with the number 2 and a colon ("2:"), to differentiate these rules from other Supreme Court rules. Apart from this preface, the Virginia rule numbers generally track the Federal Rules of Evidence. For example, the prohibition of hearsay in Federal Rule of Evidence 802 appears in Virginia Evidence Rule 2:802; the rule governing "excited utterances" is Rule 803(2) in the federal rules and Rule 2:803(2) in Virginia. This pattern holds for the vast majority of the Virginia evidence rules.

In light of the symmetry of the Virginia and federal rules, the format of the book is straightforward. For each rule of evidence, the book sets out the full text of the federal rule, followed by the full text of the corresponding Virginia rule, followed by a section titled

"Comparison and Commentary." Consequently, anyone with a general knowledge of the federal rules (or conforming state analogues) can find Virginia's treatment of a particular evidence concept in this book by looking up the correspondingly numbered Virginia rule and vice versa. The "Comparison and Commentary" section that follows each Virginia rule: (1) analyzes salient distinctions between the text of the federal and Virginia rule; (2) describes how those textual distinctions operate in application; and (3) highlights distinctions between the rules and their respective application, that may not be apparent from the rules' text.

As Virginia Evidence Rule 2:102 makes clear, the Virginia codifiers were not authorized to change preexisting evidence law during the 2012 codification project. Consequently, departures from the pre-codification case law create uncertainty as to the content of the "real" Virginia evidence rule: is it the codified rule or the rule that appeared in the pre-codification case law? At a minimum, as the "Comparison and Commentary" to Rule 2:102 discusses, alert Virginia attorneys can argue that a rule that appears to go beyond mere codification is not, in fact, the law of Virginia. Given this opportunity for legal argument, the "Comparison and Commentary" section flags areas where the Virginia codifiers arguably went beyond Virginia case law in creating the codified rules. For example, Virginia's hearsay exception for "Statements for Purposes of Medical Treatment," Rule 2:803(4), is broader and, in at least one respect, inconsistent with pre-codification case law.

Further complicating matters, some federal rules of evidence have no Virginia analogue and vice versa. These rules are still set forth in full below, along with a "Comparison and Commentary" section discussing the resulting distinction between federal and Virginia evidence law.

In some instances, the Virginia and federal rules contain a similar provision, but the rule numbers do not align. In other circumstances, federal and Virginia rules with the same number are completely unrelated (generally where there is no Virginia analogue to a federal rule and the Virginia codifiers give the federal number to an unrelated Virginia rule). These deviations are noted. Comparisons are structured as intuitively as possible, generally bringing similar rules together for comparison, even if the rules have different numbers. Lengthy rules, such as Rule 803, are broken up into subsections for ease of comparison.

A few patterns are worth highlighting. First, the Virginia codifiers often adopt the language of the federal rules of evidence for an analogous Virginia rule where the Virginia case law appeared consistent with (or parroted) the federal rule. It is generally clear in these circumstances that the Virginia and federal rules are the same. The similarity is not always apparent, however, because the Virginia courts and codifiers almost always adopted pre-2011 federal language. This language looks different from the current federal rules because the Federal Rules of Evidence were "restyled" in 2011. When the 2011 restyling is the sole reason for differences in the respective rules' language, the substance of the federal and Virginia rules is, in fact, identical. This is because the federal restyling project explicitly left the pre-restyling substance unchanged. In some cases, however, the Virginia codifiers and courts adopted federal rule language that the federal drafters later substantively amended. In these circumstances, Virginia is left with a rule that, while once identical to the federal rule, is now distinct. These distinctions can be critically important and are noted, as pertinent, in the "Comparison and Commentary" sections. Second, the Virginia rules deviate most drastically from the federal rules when the Virginia rule is the product of a statute. Such statutory derivations are generally flagged in the official title of the Virginia rules. The "Comparison and Commentary" sections also reference (and reprint) a number of Virginia statutes that touch on evidentiary principles, but are either not completely captured within the relevant evidence rule or are not referenced at all in the evidence codification.

Throughout the Comparison and Commentary sections, readers will find occasional reference to the brief explanatory notes by the Virginia codifiers available in *A Guide to the Rules of Evidence in Virginia* published by Virginia CLE Publications, and the more lengthy notes drafted by the Advisory Committee to the Federal Rules of Evidence available in a wide array of sources.

Finally, I should say a word about the book's limitations. First, it is intended for lawyers or law students with a sophisticated understanding of either Virginia or federal evidence law. This is a comparison of the two evidence codes, not a comprehensive analysis of either one. Non-lawyers or those with only a rudimentary understanding of evidence law will find many questions left unanswered. Second, the book is short, just over 200 pages. To keep the volume manageable required analytical triage. Only major distinctions are discussed and the analysis is brief. Those seeking to understand all the nuances of Virginia or federal evidence law should consult a treatise. I recommend *The Law of Evidence in Virginia*, by Charles E. Friend and Kent Sinclair, and *Federal Evidence* by Christopher B. Mueller and Laird C. Kirkpatrick. One of the key upshots of these two caveats is that this book is NOT INTENDED, NOR SHOULD IT BE USED, AS LEGAL ADVICE. As the saying goes, a person who represents himself has a fool for a client. The sentiment continues to apply even if the fool manages to obtain a 200-page evidence guide. Every case is different and the law changes day by day. Consequently, there is no substitute for a licensed attorney conducting up-to-date research on client matters.

As both the federal and Virginia rules change, revisions of this volume will become necessary. I encourage users of the book to contact me at jbellin@wm.edu to inform me of errors or omissions.

ARTICLE I. GENERAL PROVISIONS

FED. R. EV. 101. SCOPE; DEFINITIONS

(a) Scope. These rules apply to proceedings in United States courts. The specific courts and proceedings to which the rules apply, along with exceptions, are set out in Rule 1101.

(b) Definitions. In these rules:

> (1) "civil case" means a civil action or proceeding;

> (2) "criminal case" includes a criminal proceeding;

> (3) "public office" includes a public agency;

> (4) "record" includes a memorandum, report, or data compilation;

> (5) a "rule prescribed by the Supreme Court" means a rule adopted by the Supreme Court under statutory authority; and

> (6) a reference to any kind of written material or any other medium includes electronically stored information.

VA. R. EV. 2:101. TITLE

These Rules shall be known as Virginia Rules of Evidence.

Comparison and Commentary

Prior to the 2011 federal restyling project, Federal Rule 101 consisted only of Rule 101(a). Virginia provides its version of the Rule 101(a) jurisdiction provision in the next rule, Rule 2:102 and Rule 2:1101. Rule 1103 of the federal rules mirrors Virginia's Rule 2:101, naming its rules "the Federal Rules of Evidence."

The "definitions" in Federal Rule 101(b) are a result of the restyling project. As an outgrowth of the explicitly non-substantive restyling efforts, these definitions have little impact; the Virginia rules do not include an analogous definition section, although Va. Code § 8.01-385 contains some similarly generic definitions (e.g., "court"). As noted in the Comparison and Commentary to Rule 2:1001, the absence in the Virginia rule of an analogue to Fed. R. Ev. 101(b)(6) is potentially (but probably not ultimately) significant in applying the Virginia variant of the "Best Evidence Rule."

FED. R. EV. 102. PURPOSE

These rules should be construed so as to administer every proceeding fairly, eliminate unjustifiable expense and delay, and promote the development of evidence law, to the end of ascertaining the truth and securing a just determination.

VA. R. EV. 2:102. SCOPE AND CONSTRUCTION OF THESE RULES

These Rules state the law of evidence in Virginia. They are adopted to implement established principles under the common law and not to change any established case law rendered prior to the adoption of the Rules. Common law case authority, whether decided before or after the effective date of the Rules of Evidence, may be argued to the courts and considered in interpreting and applying the Rules of Evidence. As to matters not covered by these Rules, the existing law remains in effect. Where no rule is set out on a particular topic, adoption of the Rules shall have no effect on current law or practice on that topic.

Comparison and Commentary

The Federal Rules of Evidence are one of the shining success stories in federal rulemaking. The federal rules came early to an area of the common law sorely in need of coherence and codification. As a result of this urgent need and quality craftsmanship, the federal rules were adopted in states across the nation. Virginia was not one of those states. See Hanson v. Com., 14 Va. App. 173, 1844, 16 S.E.2d 14, 21 (1992) ("We have not adopted, as have many states, a set of rules of evidence."). Virginia stuck with its judge-made, common-law rules of evidence with frequent statutory additions and swiftly became one of only a handful of jurisdictions without codified Evidence rules. Thankfully this changed in 2012, when the Virginia Supreme Court adopted the rules set forth in this volume as "the law of evidence in Virginia."

Unlike the federal rules, the Virginia codification project was solely intended as a codification of Virginia's existing common law of evidence. Consequently, while the Federal Rules of Evidence were intended to sweep away federal common law doctrine and occupy the field of non-constitutional, federal evidence law, Virginia's codification project was less ambitious. Virginia Rule 2:102 reassures practitioners and judges that the codified rules are not intended "to change any established case law."

The significance of Rule 2:102's reassurance depends on how Virginia courts react when and if they determine that a codified rule veers from "established case law." Perhaps Virginia courts will then conform the codified rule to pre-existing case law either through judicial decree or formal amendment. But if the Virginia courts act too aggressively in this respect, they will undermine the codification effort and the portion of Rule 2:102 declaring the codification to be "the law of evidence in Virginia." More likely, the Virginia courts will strive to embrace the codification and privilege it over the amorphous and, at times, contradictory common law that preceded it. See, e.g., Bailey v. Com., 62 Va. App. 499, 506, 749 S.E.2d 544, 547 (2013) (relying "upon the relevant [codified] rule for its analytical framework" even while noting that the rule does not apply because the trial occurred before 2012).

FED. R. EV. 103. RULINGS ON EVIDENCE

(a) Preserving a Claim of Error. A party may claim error in a ruling to admit or exclude evidence only if the error affects a substantial right of the party and:

(1) if the ruling admits evidence, a party, on the record:

(A) timely objects or moves to strike; and

(B) states the specific ground, unless it was apparent from the context; or

(2) if the ruling excludes evidence, a party informs the court of its substance by an offer of proof, unless the substance was apparent from the context.

(b) Not Needing to Renew an Objection or Offer of Proof. Once the court rules definitively on the record--either before or at trial--a party need not renew an objection or offer of proof to preserve a claim of error for appeal.

(c) Court's Statement About the Ruling; Directing an Offer of Proof. The court may make any statement about the character or form of the evidence, the objection made, and the ruling. The court may direct that an offer of proof be made in question-and-answer form.

(d) Preventing the Jury from Hearing Inadmissible Evidence. To the extent practicable, the court must conduct a jury trial so that inadmissible evidence is not suggested to the jury by any means.

(e) Taking Notice of Plain Error. A court may take notice of a plain error affecting a substantial right, even if the claim of error was not properly preserved.

VA. R. EV. 2:103. OBJECTIONS AND PROFFERS

(a) Admission or exclusion of evidence. Error may not be predicated upon admission or exclusion of evidence, unless:

(1) As to evidence admitted, a contemporaneous objection is stated with reasonable certainty as required in Rule 5:25

and 5A:18 or in any continuing objection on the record to a related series of questions, answers or exhibits if permitted by the trial court in order to avoid the necessity of repetitious objections; or

(2) As to evidence excluded, the substance of the evidence was made known to the court by proffer.

(b) Hearing of jury. In jury cases, proceedings shall be conducted so as to prevent inadmissible evidence from being made known to the jury.

Comparison and Commentary

Both the Virginia and federal rules require a party appealing an evidentiary ruling to have initially raised an objection with the trial court. Both rules address the necessity of repeating an already-stated objection. Both rules also contain a provision directing the trial court to resolve evidentiary issues outside the jury's notice.

The federal rule directs courts to sustain an appellate challenge to an evidentiary ruling only if the ruling affected a "substantial right" of the complaining party. The federal rule follows this command with the statement that "plain error affecting a substantial right" is cognizable even if "not properly preserved." Virginia does not include either provision. The language in the federal rule essentially builds a "harmless error" standard into the evidence code, a provision found throughout state and federal appellate law.

Virginia similarly applies harmless error principles in this context even though these principles are not built into the evidence code itself. See Ferguson v. Com., 396 S.E.2d 675 (Va. 1990) (citing Va. Code § 8.01-678 for principle that "harmless-error review [is] required in all cases"); Cousins v. Com., 56 Va. App. 257, 275, 693 S.E.2d 283, 292 (2010) (reviewing claim of improper limit on cross examination for harmless error, and noting that "[i]n all cases in which we determine error has occurred, 'harmless-error review [is] required'"). Virginia law also recognizes a "plain error" standard that enables relief when justice requires even if the error was not preserved by objection. See Va. Sup. Ct. Rules, Rule 5:25 ("No ruling of the trial court, ... will be considered as a basis for reversal unless an objection was stated with reasonable certainty at the time of the ruling, except for good cause shown or to enable this Court to attain the ends of justice."); Rule 5A:18 (same). These "plain error" provisions are cross-referenced in Rule 2:103(a)(1). See also Va. Code § 19.2-324.1 (reiterating harmless error principle with respect to erroneously admitted evidence).

Federal and Virginia appellate courts review evidentiary rulings under the deferential "abuse of discretion" standard. Branham v. Com., 283 Va. 273, 281, 720 S.E.2d 74, 78 (2012); United States v. Taylor, 754 F.3d 217, 226 (4th Cir. 2014).

Fed. R. Ev. 104. Preliminary Questions

(a) In General. The court must decide any preliminary question about whether a witness is qualified, a privilege exists, or evidence is admissible. In so deciding, the court is not bound by evidence rules, except those on privilege.

(b) Relevance That Depends on a Fact. When the relevance of evidence depends on whether a fact exists, proof must be introduced sufficient to support a finding that the fact does exist. The court may admit the proposed evidence on the condition that the proof be introduced later.

(c) Conducting a Hearing So That the Jury Cannot Hear It. The court must conduct any hearing on a preliminary question so that the jury cannot hear it if:

(1) the hearing involves the admissibility of a confession;

(2) a defendant in a criminal case is a witness and so requests; or

(3) justice so requires.

(d) Cross-Examining a Defendant in a Criminal Case. By testifying on a preliminary question, a defendant in a criminal case does not become subject to cross-examination on other issues in the case.

(e) Evidence Relevant to Weight and Credibility. This rule does not limit a party's right to introduce before the jury evidence that is relevant to the weight or credibility of other evidence.

VA. R. EV. 2:104. PRELIMINARY DETERMINATIONS

(a) Determinations made by the court. The qualification of a person to be a witness, the existence of a privilege, or the admissibility of evidence shall be decided by the court, subject to the provisions of subdivision (b).

(b) Relevancy conditioned on proof of connecting facts. Whenever the relevancy of evidence depends upon proof of connecting facts, the court may admit the evidence upon or, in the court's discretion, subject to, the introduction of proof sufficient to support a finding of the connecting facts.

(c) Hearing of jury. Hearings on the admissibility of confessions in all criminal cases shall be conducted out of the hearing of the jury. Hearings on other preliminary matters in all cases shall be so conducted whenever a statute, rule, case law or the interests of justice require, or when an accused is a witness and so requests.

(d) Testimony by accused. The accused does not, by testifying upon a preliminary matter, become subject to cross-examination as to other issues in the case.

(e) Evidence of weight or credibility. This rule does not limit the right of any party to introduce before the jury evidence relevant to weight or credibility.

Comparison and Commentary

Both the Virginia and federal rules include a provision concerning the resolution of preliminary evidentiary questions. The provisions are essentially identical. Federal Rule 104(a)'s proviso that the trial court is not bound in preliminary determinations by the evidence rules, save privilege, is absent from the Virginian counterpart, but covered instead in Virginia Rule 2:1101(b).

Rule 104(b) concerns the problem of "conditional relevance," a problem widely viewed in academic circles as indistinguishable from the broader question of relevance. See Vaughn Ball, *The Myth of Conditional Relevancy*, 14 Ga. L. Rev. 435 (1980). If rules addressing conditional relevance are a conceptual mistake, the Virginia and federal rules make the same mistake, as both contain identical conditional relevance provisions.

The federal Supreme Court has filled in the requisite standard of proof for Rule 104(b) questions, stating that the proffered evidence must be sufficient for a jury to find the conditional fact by a "preponderance of the evidence." Huddleston v. U.S., 485 U.S. 681, 690 (1988) ("The court simply examines all the evidence in the case and decides whether the jury could reasonably find the conditional fact ... by a preponderance of the evidence.") Left unsaid, but indisputable is that because the relevance question is ultimately for the jury, the proffered evidence must be admissible. Neither Virginia case law nor the codification commentary expressly adopt the preponderance standard, but there does not appear to be a competing standard in the Virginia case law and the Virginia Supreme Court has signaled acquiescence in the federal standard, citing *Huddleston* in this context in Prieto v. Com., 283 Va. 149, 172, 721 S.E.2d 484, 498 (2012).

Both rules state, in subsection (c), that sensitive preliminary evidentiary questions should be determined outside the presence of the jury. Other provisions of the rules are identical.

FED. R. EV. 105. LIMITING EVIDENCE THAT IS NOT ADMISSIBLE AGAINST OTHER PARTIES OR FOR OTHER PURPOSES

If the court admits evidence that is admissible against a party or for a purpose--but not against another party or for another purpose--the court, on timely request, must restrict the evidence to its proper scope and instruct the jury accordingly.

VA. R. EV. 2:105. PROOF ADMITTED FOR LIMITED PURPOSES

When evidence is admissible as to one party or for one purpose but not admissible as to another party or for another purpose, the court upon motion shall restrict such evidence to its proper scope and instruct the jury accordingly. The court may give such limiting instructions sua sponte, to which any party may object.

Comparison and Commentary

The federal and Virginia rules governing limiting instructions are the same, except that the Virginia provision makes explicit allowance for judges to give limiting instructions on their own initiative. Despite the omission of such a statement from the federal rule, federal courts are empowered to instruct sua sponte and may, in rare circumstances, even be obligated to do so. United States v. Brawner, 32 F.3d 602, 605 (D.C. Cir. 1994) (acknowledging language of Rule 105, but stating "[w]e have nonetheless held that the failure of a district judge to offer a limiting instruction to the defendant sua sponte may constitute reversible error").

FED. R. EV. 106. REMAINDER OF OR RELATED WRITINGS OR RECORDED STATEMENTS

If a party introduces all or part of a writing or recorded statement, an adverse party may require the introduction, at that time, of any other part--or any other writing or recorded statement--that in fairness ought to be considered at the same time.

VA. R. EV. 2:106. REMAINDER OF A WRITING OR RECORDED STATEMENT (Rule 2:106(b) derived from Code § 8.01-417.1)

(a) Related Portions of a Writing in Civil and Criminal Cases. When part of a writing or recorded statement is introduced by a party, upon motion by another party the court may require the offering party to introduce any other part of the writing or recorded statement which ought in fairness to be considered contemporaneously with it, unless such additional portions are inadmissible under the Rules of Evidence.

(b) Lengthy Documents in Civil cases. To expedite trials in civil cases, upon timely motion, the court may permit the reading to the jury, or the introduction into evidence, of relevant portions of lengthy and complex documents without the necessity of having the jury hear or receive the entire document. The court, in its discretion, may permit the entire document to be received by the jury, or may order the parties to edit from any such document admitted into evidence information that is irrelevant to the proceedings.

Comparison and Commentary

Both the federal and Virginia rules include a "rule of completeness" that permits the admission of the remainder of a recorded statement, already partially entered into evidence, when fairness dictates. The Virginia provision adds an important codicil -- "unless such additional portions are inadmissible under the Rules of Evidence" -- to its rule. This codicil places Virginia firmly on one side of a longstanding federal circuit split on the question of whether Rule 106 is merely a proof-ordering provision or a powerful trump of other evidence rules. See Andrea N. Kochert, *The Admission of Hearsay Through Rule 106: And Now You Know the Rest of the Story*, 46 Ind. L. Rev. 499, 509 (2013) (cataloguing circuit split).

By its terms, Virginia's rule 2:106 is merely an ordering principle, permitting a party to introduce otherwise admissible portions of a document or recording "contemporaneously" with the portions introduced by the opposing party. For example, if the defendant's recorded confession stated, "I was angry, so I shot him ... a dirty look" and the prosecution introduced just the portion before the ellipses, Rule 106 would allow the defense to compel introduction of the portion following the ellipses (if otherwise admissible) during the prosecution's case.

In the federal system, a substantial number of the circuits grant Rule 106 a more robust role than the mere order-of-proof principle codified in Virginia. Kochert, supra, at 507 (noting that the First, Second, Seventh, Tenth, Eleventh, and D.C. Circuits adopt the position that Rule 106 trumps other evidence rules); 2 Jones on Evidence § 11:39 (7th ed.) (recognizing as the "better view" that the "'rule of completeness' permits introduction of otherwise inadmissible evidence for the limited purposes of explaining or putting other, already admitted evidence, into context, or avoiding misleading the jury"). These courts read Rule 106 to permit the introduction of "otherwise inadmissible evidence" if fairness so dictates. United States v. Sutton, 801 F.2d 1346, 1368 (D.C. Cir. 1986) ("Rule 106 can adequately fulfill its function only by permitting the admission of some otherwise inadmissible evidence when the court finds in fairness that the proffered evidence should be

11

considered contemporaneously.") Fourth Circuit decisions are inconsistent on the question. Kochert, supra, at 507.

While Virginia's codification takes this point on directly, Virginia's case law is less emphatic. In fact, there is a line of cases regarding defendant confessions that appears inconsistent with the codification. Compare Brown v. Com., 36 Va. 633, 634 (Va. Gen. Ct. 1838) ("When the confession of a party, either in a civil or criminal case (for the rule is the same in both) is given in evidence, the whole, as well that part which makes for him as that which is against him, must be taken together and go to the jury as evidence in the case.") with Codification Commentary to Rule 2:106 ("if a defendant provided police with a written confession to a crime, in which he also advanced certain mitigating circumstances regarding the crime, the self-serving portions of the statement would not necessarily be admitted simply because the portion confessing to the crime is admitted"); see also Pierce v. Com., 2 Va. App. 383, 391, 345 S.E.2d 1, 5 (1986) (recognizing principle announced in *Brown*, supra, but holding that it did not apply where a portion of the defendant's statement "does not bear on any element of the crime and, ..., is not probative of any issue").

Neither the federal nor the Virginia rule applies beyond recordings or documents, to testimony about oral conversations or analogous evidence. See Advisory Committee Note to Fed. R. Evid. 106.

Subparagraph (b) of the Virginia rule reprints a Virginia Code provision that allows excerpts from larger documents to be admitted in civil trials. See Va. Code § 8.01-417.1. The federal evidence rules do not have a similar provision. See also Va. Sup. Ct. Rule 4:7(a)(5) (same rule for depositions).

ARTICLE II. JUDICIAL NOTICE

FED. R. EV. 201. JUDICIAL NOTICE OF ADJUDICATIVE FACTS

(a) Scope. This rule governs judicial notice of an adjudicative fact only, not a legislative fact.

(b) Kinds of Facts That May Be Judicially Noticed. The court may judicially notice a fact that is not subject to reasonable dispute because it:

(1) is generally known within the trial court's territorial jurisdiction; or

(2) can be accurately and readily determined from sources whose accuracy cannot reasonably be questioned.

(c) Taking Notice. The court:

(1) may take judicial notice on its own; or

(2) must take judicial notice if a party requests it and the court is supplied with the necessary information.

(d) Timing. The court may take judicial notice at any stage of the proceeding.

(e) Opportunity to Be Heard. On timely request, a party is entitled to be heard on the propriety of taking judicial notice and the nature of the fact to be noticed. If the court takes judicial notice before notifying a party, the party, on request, is still entitled to be heard.

(f) Instructing the Jury. In a civil case, the court must instruct the jury to accept the noticed fact as conclusive. In a criminal case, the court must instruct the jury that it may or may not accept the noticed fact as conclusive.

VA. R. EV. 2:201. JUDICIAL NOTICE OF ADJUDICATIVE FACTS

(a) Notice. A court may take judicial notice of a factual matter not subject to reasonable dispute in that it is either (1) common knowledge or (2) capable of accurate and ready determination by resort to sources whose accuracy cannot reasonably be questioned.

(b) Time of taking notice. Judicial notice may be taken at any stage of the proceeding.

(c) Opportunity to be heard. A party is entitled upon timely motion to an opportunity to be heard as to the propriety of taking judicial notice.

Comparison and Commentary

Both the federal and Virginia rules include a provision governing judicial notice. The provisions are basically identical. The only major textual distinction in the overlapping portions of the rules is that Virginia replaces the federal rule's phrase, "is generally known within the trial court's territorial jurisdiction" with "common knowledge." It is unlikely that the different terminology communicates any substantive difference between the two rules; the distinction likely reflects the more diverse geographic span of the federal system.

The federal rule specifically allows a court to take judicial notice "on its own" motion, while the Virginia rule is silent on the question. The Virginia courts are presumably permitted to take judicial notice without prompting, assuming adequate provision of notice to the parties. See State Farm v. Powell, 227 Va. 492, 497, 318 S.E.2d 393, 395 (Va. 1984) (criticizing trial court for taking judicial notice of certain facts, but not suggesting any impropriety of doing so on its own initiative); Com. v. McLaughlin, 49 Va. Cir. 571 (Va. Cir. 1998) ("I suppose the Court could, on it own motion, take judicial notice of a matter, but the Court should announce such notice and make it a part of the record in the case."). If all else fails, a trial court could simply indicate its amenability to a request to take judicial notice, prompting a request from the benefited party.

Another distinction is that Virginia's rule does not include a provision regarding instructing the jury on the weight to be given to judicially noticed facts. The case law is similarly silent on this issue. Nevertheless, it is likely that Virginia courts would follow the procedures set out in the federal rule, particularly with respect to the non-preclusive nature of judicial notice in criminal cases. It is also clear that a Virginia court must inform the jury of the facts judicially noticed for the exercise to have any significance; absent their presentation to the jury, judicially noticed facts will not be "imputed to a jury." Thomas v. Com., 48 Va.App. 605, 609-10, 633 S.E.2d 229, 232 (Va. App. 2006) (citing Fed. R. Ev. 201).

The federal rule specifically distinguishes between "adjudicative" and "legislative" facts. See Castillo-Villagra v. I.N.S., 972 F.2d 1017, 1026 (9th Cir. 1992) ("Professor Kenneth Culp Davis distinguished between adjudicative facts, which are those concerning the immediate parties, and legislative facts, which help the tribunal determine law and policy and are ordinarily general facts not concerning the immediate parties.") (citing Kenneth Culp Davis, *Judicial Notice*, 55 Colum. L. Rev. 945, 952 (1955)). The Virginia rule, while labeled "Judicial Notice of Adjudicative Facts," does not reference the adjudicative/legislative distinction in its text. There is no indication in the commentary or the case law, however, that the failure to limit the rule to adjudicative facts means that other facts (e.g., legislative facts) fall under Virginia's rule. In fact, Virginia has a separate judicial notice rule that covers a quintessential legislative fact -- the law -- in Rule 2:202. See Com. v. Johnson, 85-CR-10, 1985 WL 306863 (Va. Cir. 1985) (unpublished) (describing "[t]he process of interpreting the law" as "judicial notice of 'legislative facts,'" and distinguishing that from "'adjudicative facts' - i.e., facts in issue in the particular case").

VA. R. EV. 2:202. JUDICIAL NOTICE OF LAW (derived from Code §§ 8.01-386 and 19.2-265.2)

(a) Notice To Be Taken. Whenever, in any civil or criminal case it becomes necessary to ascertain what the law, statutory, administrative, or otherwise, of this Commonwealth, of another state, of the United States, of another country, or of any political subdivision or agency of the same, or under an applicable treaty or international convention is, or was, at any time, the court shall take judicial notice thereof whether specially pleaded or not.

(b) Sources of Information. The court, in taking such notice, shall in a criminal case and may in a civil case consult any book, record, register, journal, or other official document or publication purporting to contain, state, or explain such law, and may consider any evidence or other information or argument that is offered on the subject.

Comparison and Commentary

Virginia's code includes a specific rule governing judicial notice of one type of "legislative fact," the content of the law. The provision provides courts with virtually unlimited discretion to seek out and ascertain "the law." The federal rules do not include such a provision; instead judicial notice of the law is unregulated under the federal rules along with judicial notice of other non-adjudicative facts.

VA. R. EV. 2:203. JUDICIAL NOTICE OF OFFICIAL PUBLICATIONS (derived from Code § 8.01-388)

The court shall take judicial notice of the contents of all official publications of the Commonwealth and its political subdivisions and agencies required to be published pursuant to the laws thereof, and of all such official publications of other states, of the United States, of other countries, and of the political subdivisions and agencies of each published within those jurisdictions pursuant to the laws thereof.

Comparison and Commentary

Virginia's rules provide a sweeping, statute-derived, provision for taking judicial notice of "official publications" of Virginia's agencies as well as those of other states and countries. The commentary to the codified rule wisely cautions that this provision "does not address the question" whether such documents are to receive "any binding effect" – presumably not! – or "hearsay aspects" of the contents of such publications. There is sparse case law on this provision. The case law that does exist, however, suggests that this evidence provision is amenable to significant mischief. Scafetta v. Arlington County, , 13 Va. App. 646, 648, 414 S.E.2d 438, 439 (Va. App. 1992) on reh'g, 14 Va. App. 834, 425 S.E.2d 807 (Va. App. 1992) (concluding that judge could take judicial notice of facts contained in official publication whether or not "the document me[]t the requirements for admissibility into evidence"). The Codification Commentary suggests, however, that the judicial notice provision operates merely as an authentication provision, allowing the parties to introduce official documents, without calling the officials who prepared or produced them. Under this view, the introducing party would still be required to establish that the documents (and their contents) are otherwise admissible, and the factfinder could give such weight to the noticed materials as it deems appropriate.

ARTICLE III. PRESUMPTIONS

FED. R. EV. 301. PRESUMPTIONS IN CIVIL CASES GENERALLY

In a civil case, unless a federal statute or these rules provide otherwise, the party against whom a presumption is directed has the burden of producing evidence to rebut the presumption. But this rule does not shift the burden of persuasion, which remains on the party who had it originally.

VA. R. EV. 2:301. PRESUMPTIONS IN GENERAL IN CIVIL ACTIONS AND PROCEEDINGS

Unless otherwise provided by Virginia common law or statute, in a civil action a rebuttable presumption imposes on the party against whom it is directed the burden of going forward with evidence to rebut or meet the presumption, but does not shift to such party the burden of proof, which remains throughout the trial upon the party on whom it originally rested.

Comparison and Commentary

The Virginia and Federal rules respecting presumptions are identical; distinctions arise from the Virginia codifiers' reliance on the unrestyled federal rule and insertion of "rebuttable," a qualifier that is otherwise implicit in the rule's reference to rebutting the presumption. Neither the Virginia nor the federal rules provide for presumptions in criminal cases, likely due to doubts about the constitutionality of such presumptions. See Francis v. Franklin, 471 U.S. 307, 314 (1985).

Fed. R. Ev. 302. Applying State Law to Presumptions in Civil Cases

In a civil case, state law governs the effect of a presumption regarding a claim or defense for which state law supplies the rule of decision.

Va. R. Ev. 2:302. Applicability of Federal Law in Civil Actions and Proceedings

The effect of a presumption is determined by federal law in any civil action or proceeding as to which federal law supplies the rule of decision.

Comparison and Commentary

Both the Virginia and federal rule state, in similar terms, that the effect of a presumption will be determined by the rules of the respective jurisdiction (state or federal) that supplies the underlying rule of decision.

ARTICLE IV. RELEVANCE, POLICY AND CHARACTER

FED. R. EV. 401. TEST FOR RELEVANT EVIDENCE

Evidence is relevant if:

(a) it has any tendency to make a fact more or less probable than it would be without the evidence; and

(b) the fact is of consequence in determining the action.

VA. R. EV. 2:401. DEFINITION OF "RELEVANT EVIDENCE"

"Relevant evidence" means evidence having any tendency to make the existence of any fact in issue more probable or less probable than it would be without the evidence.

Comparison and Commentary

Since court and juror time is a finite commodity, every jurisdiction prohibits irrelevant evidence. Virginia's definition of relevance is essentially the same as the federal definition. In fact, Virginia's rule precisely tracks the language of the unrevised federal rule, with one exception. The Virginia rule substitutes "fact in issue" for "fact of consequence in determining the action." One might read this change to suggest that the Virginia rule limits relevance to disputed facts, contrary to the federal rule. See Adv. Committee Notes, Fed. R. Ev. 401 ("The fact to which the evidence is directed need not be in dispute."). There is no indication in Virginia case law or the commentary to the codification that such a distinction is intended. Instead, it appears that the substitution of "fact in issue" for "fact of consequence" has no substantive significance. As a result, background facts and the like are "relevant" in Virginia as in the federal system even if there is no dispute as to their accuracy. See

Smith v. Com., 219 Va. 455, 468, 248 S.E.2d 135, 143 (Va. 1978) (acknowledging that challenged testimony "did nothing more than supplement the testimonial narrative of the sequence of events preceding and following the commission of the crime," and "though not directly relevant to the question of guilt," was nonetheless "material to the fact-finder's understanding of the crucial event"). In fact, one of the more commonly cited Virginia cases on the definition of relevance, Thomas v. Com., 44 Va.App. 741, 754, 607 S.E.2d 738, 744 (Va. App. 2005), blends the "in issue" and "of consequence" phrases while quoting the Federal definition: "It is universally recognized that evidence, to be relevant to an inquiry, need not conclusively prove the ultimate fact in issue, but only have 'any tendency to make the existence of any fact that is of consequence to the determination of the action more probable or less probable than it would be without the evidence.'" Id. at 744 (quoting McKoy v. North Carolina, 494 U.S. 433, 440 (1990) and Fed. R. Ev. 401).

FED. R. EV. 402. GENERAL ADMISSIBILITY OF RELEVANT EVIDENCE

Relevant evidence is admissible unless any of the following provides otherwise:

- the United States Constitution;

- a federal statute;

- these rules; or

- other rules prescribed by the Supreme Court.

Irrelevant evidence is not admissible.

VA. R. EV. 2:402. RELEVANT EVIDENCE GENERALLY ADMISSIBLE; IRRELEVANT EVIDENCE INADMISSIBLE

(a) General Principle. All relevant evidence is admissible,

except as otherwise provided by the Constitution of the United States, the Constitution of Virginia, statute, Rules of the Supreme Court of Virginia, or other evidentiary principles. Evidence that is not relevant is not admissible.

(b) Results of Polygraph Examinations. The results of polygraph examinations are not admissible.

Comparison and Commentary

Both the Virginia and federal rules permit relevant evidence unless trumped by other rules, and bar irrelevant evidence. (Rule 401 defines relevance). The Virginia rule barring irrelevant evidence also prohibits the results of "polygraph examinations." Rule 2:402(b). The Federal Rules do not include any specific prohibition of lie detector evidence. Still, the federal courts find ample support for excluding lie detector test results in various generally applicable evidence rules, and primarily Rule 702 (requiring expert testimony to be based on reliable principles). It is unclear why the Virginia codifiers did not follow this same approach, and instead included a specific bar to polygraph evidence in the evidence code. The Virginia case law's prohibition of lie detector evidence parallels the federal one, excluding such evidence on reliability rather than relevance grounds. See Odum v. Com., 225 Va. 123, 132, 301 S.E.2d 145, 150 (Va. 1983) ("In Virginia, results of lie detector tests are not viewed as scientifically reliable, and we have held that the exclusion of such findings, even though favorable to the accused, was proper."). The codifiers' inflexible approach may become salient if and when a Virginia court is presented with reliable lie detection evidence. Contrast Lee v. Com., 200 Va. 233, 237, 105 S.E.2d 152, 155 (Va. 1958) ("such tests generally have not *as yet* been proved scientifically reliable") (emphasis added) with Rule 2:402(b) ("The results of polygraph examinations are not admissible.") A prohibition, as in the federal courts, that is the based on doubts as to scientific reliability gives way upon a showing of sufficient scientific advancement. A prohibition without limitation, like that contained in Rule 2:402(b), does not.

Although not cited by the Virginia codifiers, the Virginia Code does include a provision titled, "Evidence of polygraph examination inadmissible in any proceeding." Va. Code § 8.01-418.2. The awkwardly worded provision, however, appears to apply only to employee grievance proceedings, and has been referenced to date in only a single, unpublished case. See Lee v. Southside Virginia Training Ctr., No. 0976-09-2, 2010 WL 342592, at *2 (Va. Ct. App. 2010) ("Code § 8.01–418.2 prohibits the admission of 'the analysis of any polygraph test charts produced during any polygraph examination administered to a party ...' in a state grievance proceeding.")

FED. R. EV. 403. EXCLUDING RELEVANT EVIDENCE FOR PREJUDICE, CONFUSION, WASTE OF TIME, OR OTHER REASONS

The court may exclude relevant evidence if its probative value is substantially outweighed by a danger of one or more of the following: unfair prejudice, confusing the issues, misleading the jury, undue delay, wasting time, or needlessly presenting cumulative evidence.

VA. R. EV. 2:403. EXCLUSION OF RELEVANT EVIDENCE ON GROUNDS OF PREJUDICE, CONFUSION, MISLEADING THE JURY, OR NEEDLESS PRESENTATION OF CUMULATIVE EVIDENCE

Relevant evidence may be excluded if:

(a) the probative value of the evidence is substantially outweighed by (i) the danger of unfair prejudice, or (ii) its likelihood of confusing or misleading the trier of fact; or

(b) the evidence is needlessly cumulative.

Comparison and Commentary

Both the Virginia and federal rules grant the trial court discretion to exclude relevant evidence when its probative value is substantially outweighed by certain dangers. The only distinction in the respective rules' text is that the Virginia rule omits "undue delay" and "wasting time" as grounds for exclusion. However, these provisions in the federal rule are somewhat redundant and Virginia courts can always point to principles of relevance and cumulativeness to cover precisely the same ground. Cf. Smith v. Ellis, 22 Va. Cir. 422 (Va. Cir. 1991) ("Evidence may be excluded if its probative value is substantially outweighed by the danger of unfair prejudice, waste of time, confusion of the issues, or needless presentation of misleading facts.")

FED. R. EV. 404. CHARACTER EVIDENCE; CRIMES OR OTHER ACTS

(a) Character Evidence.

(1) Prohibited Uses. Evidence of a person's character or character trait is not admissible to prove that on a particular occasion the person acted in accordance with the character or trait.

(2) Exceptions for a Defendant or Victim in a Criminal Case. The following exceptions apply in a criminal case:

(A) a defendant may offer evidence of the defendant's pertinent trait, and if the evidence is admitted, the prosecutor may offer evidence to rebut it;

(B) subject to the limitations in Rule 412, a defendant may offer evidence of an alleged victim's pertinent trait, and if the evidence is admitted, the prosecutor may:

> (i) offer evidence to rebut it; and

> (ii) offer evidence of the defendant's same trait; and

(C) in a homicide case, the prosecutor may offer evidence of the alleged victim's trait of peacefulness to rebut evidence that the victim was the first aggressor.

(3) **Exceptions for a Witness.** Evidence of a witness's character may be admitted under Rules 607, 608, and 609.

(b) **Crimes, Wrongs, or Other Acts.**

(1) **Prohibited Uses.** Evidence of a crime, wrong, or other act is not admissible to prove a person's character in order to show that on a particular occasion the person acted in accordance with the character.

(2) **Permitted Uses; Notice in a Criminal Case.** This evidence may be admissible for another purpose, such as proving motive, opportunity, intent, preparation, plan, knowledge, identity, absence of mistake, or lack of accident. On request by a defendant in a criminal case, the prosecutor must:

> (A) provide reasonable notice of the general nature of any such evidence that the prosecutor intends to offer at trial; and

> (B) do so before trial--or during trial if the court, for good cause, excuses lack of pretrial notice.

VA. R. Ev. 2:404. CHARACTER EVIDENCE NOT ADMISSIBLE TO PROVE CONDUCT; EXCEPTIONS; OTHER CRIMES

(a) Character evidence generally. Evidence of a person's character or character trait is not admissible for the purpose of proving action in conformity therewith on a particular occasion, except:

> (1) Character trait of accused. Evidence of a pertinent character trait of the accused offered by the accused, or by the prosecution to rebut the same;

> (2) Character trait of victim. Except as provided in Rule 2:412, evidence of a pertinent character trait or acts of violence by the victim of the crime offered by an accused who has adduced evidence of self defense, or by the prosecution (i) to rebut defense evidence, or (ii) in a criminal case when relevant as circumstantial evidence to establish the death of the victim when other evidence is unavailable; or

> (3) Character trait of witness. Evidence of the character trait of a witness, as provided in Rules 2:607, 2:608, and 2:609.

(b) Other crimes, wrongs, or acts. Except as provided in Rule 2:413 or by statute, evidence of other crimes, wrongs, or acts is generally not admissible to prove the character trait of a person in order to show that the person acted in conformity therewith. However, if the legitimate probative value of such proof outweighs its incidental prejudice, such evidence is admissible if it tends to prove any relevant fact pertaining to the offense charged, such as where it is relevant to show motive, opportunity, intent, preparation, plan, knowledge, identity, absence of mistake, accident, or if they are part of a common scheme or plan.

Comparison and Commentary

The federal and Virginia rules continue the longstanding common-law tradition of generally prohibiting evidence of a person's character or past conduct offered to show the subject's propensity to act in a certain manner. See Kirkpatrick v. Com., 211 Va. 269, 272, 176 S.E.2d 802, 805 (Va. 1970) ("evidence of other offenses should be excluded if offered merely for the purpose of showing that the accused was likely to commit the crime charged in the indictment"); Michelson v. U.S., 335 U.S. 469, 475 (1948) ("Courts that follow the common-law tradition almost unanimously have come to disallow resort by the prosecution to any kind of evidence of a defendant's evil character to establish a probability of his guilt.")

Evidence of Other Acts Offered for Non-Propensity Purposes

The Virginia and federal rules follow a similar pattern: evidence is prohibited if its probative force comes from the forbidden propensity inference; evidence is not prohibited if it is relevant for some other purpose. The rules also provide similar illustrations of other purposes, such as to prove "motive, opportunity, intent," etc.

There are textual differences worth noting. Under the federal rule, it is clear that evidence that proves something like "identity" via propensity (e.g., an argument that a defendant charged with robbery, who claims mistaken identity, is more likely the perpetrator because he was previously convicted of robbery), is barred by Rule 404. Such evidence does go to identity, but it is inadmissible because it is not being offered for "another purpose," i.e., a purpose other than propensity. The Virginia rule is less clear on this point. First, there is a caveat in Rule 2:404(b) ("generally not admissible") not found in the federal rule. Second, Virginia's rule does not characterize the permitted use of the evidence as "another purpose"; instead, the Virginia rule states that such evidence is allowed if it "prove[s] any relevant fact pertaining to the offense charged, such as where it is relevant to show motive, opportunity, intent…." This leaves open the question of whether a Virginia litigant can validly argue that evidence is admissible when it proves a relevant fact such as identity, motive, etc., but only does so through propensity reasoning. See Com. v. Minor, 267 Va. 166, 174, 591 S.E.2d 61, 66-67 (Va. 2004) ("[I]f the evidence of other similar offenses had been offered as proof on a contested issue about the defendant's identity in these offenses, that evidence would likely have been admissible."). Despite this uncertainty, the answer under Virginia law is probably that such indirect-propensity reasoning is not permitted, and loose language in the rule and case law should not be read to support a contrary position. After all, allowing evidence of character and other bad acts to show identity, etc., through propensity, eviscerates the general prohibition of character evidence. See Rose v. Com., 270 Va. 3, 10, 613 S.E.2d 454, 458 (Va. 2005) (rejecting evidence that defendant committed uncharged robbery where similarities between past and charged robbery were not "so distinctive or idiosyncratic that the fact finder reasonably could infer that the same person committed both crimes"); Boyd v. Com., 213 Va. 52, 53, 189 S.E.2d 359, 360 (Va. 1972) (reversing conviction where trial court allowed testimony about defendant's prior uncharged drug sales as "part of a general scheme, of which the crime charged is a part"). As a result, the Virginia and federal rule likely have the same meaning on this critical point despite the textual differences noted above. These differences do, however, make it more likely that Virginia courts could mistakenly permit propensity evidence because it was offered to establish "identity, motive, absence of mistake," etc.

Another distinction is that Virginia Rule 2:404(b) includes a mini-Rule 403 proviso as a last line of exclusion for evidence that otherwise complies with Rule 404. This internal balancing test (exclusion required if "incidental prejudice" outweighs "legitimate probative value") is more likely to exclude than the default 403 balance (exclusion required if unfair prejudice *substantially* outweighs probative value). As a consequence, Virginia's rule, as written, makes the introduction of other crimes evidence more difficult than it is under the federal rules. Indeed, this proviso may be intended to counteract the relative laxity of Virginia's propensity prohibition discussed above.

As a result of a 1991 amendment, the federal rule imposes a "reasonable notice" requirement on prosecutors seeking to offer other acts for a non-propensity purpose. The Virginia rule does not include a notice requirement. In capital sentencing hearings, a separate statute requires the prosecution to provide "notice in writing" of any "unadjudicated criminal conduct" sought to be offered. Va. Code § 19.2-264.3:2.

Exceptions to the Character Prohibition

Both the Virginia and federal rules provide an exception to the propensity ban when the defendant offers evidence of his own character, or the victim's character, or when any party offers evidence regarding a witness' character.

The federal and Virginia provisions differ in three ways with respect to the defendant's ability to offer evidence about the victim's character. First, the Virginia rule does not authorize the prosecution to respond to defense evidence about a victim's character trait by offering "evidence of the defendant's same trait." This provision added by a 2000 amendment to the federal rule is absent from the Virginia rule. Second, the Virginia rule provides that a defendant claiming self-defense can introduce "acts of violence by the victim of the crime" – whereas under the federal rules, Rule 405 allows only reputation or opinion evidence, limiting the use of specific acts to questioning on cross-examination. The Virginia provision comes directly from the case law. See Edwards v. Com., 10 Va. App. 140, 142, 390 S.E.2d 204, 206 (Va. App. 1990) ("Where the defendant claims self defense, evidence of prior acts of violence by the victim is relevant as bearing on the reasonable apprehension which the defendant may have experienced *and on the likelihood of the victim's aggressive behavior* as claimed by the defendant.") (emphasis added). The italicized portion of the quote from *Edwards* makes clear that such evidence is permissible as propensity evidence. Third, the Virginia rule permits the introduction of evidence of a victim's character "in a criminal case when relevant as circumstantial evidence to establish the death of the victim when other evidence is unavailable." This provision comes from the case of Epperly v. Com, which held the prosecution could introduce evidence of the victim's (good) character to show "the unlikelihood that [she] would take her own life, flee, or fall victim to accidental death because of some dangerous habit or practice." 224 Va. 214, 230, 294 S.E.2d 882, 891 (Va. 1982). The *Epperly* rule appears to be very narrow, applying only when the prosecution is in the difficult position of trying to prove a murder without a body. See McCain v. Com., 5 Va. App. 81, 84, 360 S.E.2d 854, 856 (Va. App. 1987) (distinguishing *Epperly* because "the Commonwealth was not faced with the dilemma of the undiscovered body of the victim").

FED. R. EV. 405. METHODS OF PROVING CHARACTER

(a) By Reputation or Opinion. When evidence of a person's character or character trait is admissible, it may be proved by testimony about the person's reputation or by testimony in the form of an opinion. On cross-examination of the character witness, the court may allow an inquiry into relevant specific instances of the person's conduct.

(b) By Specific Instances of Conduct. When a person's character or character trait is an essential element of a charge, claim, or defense, the character or trait may also be proved by relevant specific instances of the person's conduct.

VA. R. EV. 2:405. METHODS OF PROVING CHARACTER TRAITS

(a) Reputation proof. Where evidence of a person's character trait is admissible under these Rules, proof may be made by testimony as to reputation; but a witness may not give reputation testimony except upon personal knowledge of the reputation. On cross-examination, inquiry is allowable into relevant specific instances of conduct.

(b) Specific instances of conduct. In cases in which a character trait of a person is an essential element of a charge, claim, or defense, proof may also be made of specific instances of conduct of such person on direct or cross-examination.

Comparison and Commentary

The federal and Virginia rules restrict the form that evidence about a person's character can take when such evidence is admissible. The federal rule allows witnesses testifying about character to testify as to the person's *reputation* in the community or the witness' own *opinion* of the person's character. Virginia follows the common-law tradition of allowing only testimony as to reputation; Virginia does not allow testimony in the form of a witness' personal opinion of someone's character.

The provision in the Virginia rule requiring "personal knowledge" is not included in the federal rule, but some foundation is always required for reputation testimony, so the Virginia provision seems superfluous. It may be explained by Virginia courts' expression of the principle in the context of "negative" character evidence – i.e., testimony about the absence of having heard of a certain type of reputation. See Jackson v. Com., 266 Va. 423, 440, 587 S.E.2d 532, 544 (Va. 2003) ("a witness must be aware of the party's reputation in the community before he may testify as to the lack of any reputation for a particular characteristic").

Both the federal and Virginia rules permit specific instances to be inquired into on cross-examination of the character witness; proof of specific instances is otherwise prohibited. Impeachment of a particular statement may, however, be made with specific instances. See Roy v. Com., 191 Va. 722, 722 62 S.E.2d 902, 902 (Va. 1951) (evidence contradicting defendant's claim to be ignorant of gambling admissible to impeach because "not offered to attack the [defendant's] reputation"). As discussed in the Comparison and Commentary to Rule 2:404 (above), evidence of specific acts of violence by the victim are allowed in Virginia when a defendant claims self-defense.

Both rules contain an identical, narrow exception in subsection (b) that allows proof of specific instances when proof of character is "essential" to a claim or defense.

FED. R. EV. 406. HABIT; ROUTINE PRACTICE

Evidence of a person's habit or an organization's routine practice may be admitted to prove that on a particular occasion the person or organization acted in accordance with the habit or routine practice. The court may admit this evidence regardless of whether it is corroborated or whether there was an eyewitness.

VA. R. EV. 2:406. HABIT AND ROUTINE PRACTICE IN CIVIL CASES (derived from Code § 8.01-397.1)

(a) Admissibility. In a civil case, evidence of a person's habit or of an organization's routine practice, whether corroborated or not and regardless of the presence of eyewitnesses, is relevant to prove that the conduct of the person or organization on a particular occasion conformed with the habit or routine practice. Evidence of prior conduct may be relevant to rebut evidence of habit or routine practice.

(b) Habit and routine practice defined. A "habit" is a person's regular response to repeated specific situations. A "routine practice" is a regular course of conduct of a group of persons or an organization in response to repeated specific situations.

Comparison and Commentary

Both the federal and Virginia rules include a rule addressing "habit" evidence. The federal rule allows evidence of habit ("may be admitted") in both criminal and civil cases. The Virginia rule only addresses habit evidence in civil cases. The Virginia rule includes a definition of "habit" that is not present in the federal rule, but corresponds with the description of habit provided by noted evidence scholar, Charles T. McCormick, and quoted in the Advisory Committee note to the federal rule -- "one's regular response to repeated specific situations."

The peculiarities in Virginia's habit rule are best understood in historical context. Rule 2:406 is derived from Va. Code § 8.01-397.1, which was a legislative repudiation of the Virginia Supreme Court ruling in Ligon v. Southside Cardiology Associates, 258 Va. 306, 519 S.E.2d 361 (1999). In *Ligon*, the court set aside a defense verdict in a medical malpractice lawsuit because the trial court admitted evidence of the defendant's routine practice as "habit." The *Ligon* court ruled the evidence was improperly admitted because, "[i]n a negligence action, evidence of habitual conduct is inadmissible to prove conduct at the time of the incident complained of because such evidence is collateral to the issues at trial." Id. at 312, 364. "[T]he relevant inquiry in a negligence action is not whether a defendant has a habit of compliance with the type of duty at issue, but whether the defendant breached a specific duty owed to the plaintiff at a particular time." Id.

Virginia Code § 8.01-397.1 responds to *Ligon*, tailoring its language to the specific holding of that case. The section applies only to civil cases (like *Ligon*) and commands not that evidence may be admissible (as in the federal rule), but that it is "relevant." See Va. Code § 8.01-397.1 (C) ("The provisions of this section are applicable only in civil proceedings."); Johnson v. Raviotta, 264 Va. 27, 37, 563 S.E.2d 727, 734 (2002) ("This section does no more than establish that evidence showing a certain pattern of conduct is relevant evidence and, therefore, a court cannot refuse to admit such evidence on the ground that it is collateral, irrelevant evidence.")

Virginia Rule 2:406, like § 8.01-397.1, says nothing about the admissibility of habit evidence in a criminal case. That question is governed by more generic rules (e.g., character evidence, relevance) and existing case law. The one precedent for the use of habit evidence in a criminal case is Graham v. Com., 127 Va. 808, 103 S.E. 565, 570 (Va. 1920), which rejected a challenge to the admission of evidence of the victim's habit of not using profane language. The Supreme Court attempted to cabin *Graham* in *Ligon*, suggesting in a footnote that *Graham* was an example of permissible character rather than "habit" evidence – though *Graham* itself used "habit" terminology. *Ligon* at 312, 364 n.* ("our holding in *Graham* was limited to the use of a narrow category of rebuttal testimony to a claim of self-defense in a criminal prosecution, and is unrelated to the present issue of the admissibility of habit evidence in a negligence action"); Hodges v. Com., 45 Va. App. 735, 764, 613 S.E.2d 834, 848 (2005) rev'd on other grounds, 272 Va. 418, 634 S.E.2d 680 (2006) ("existing Supreme Court precedent authorizes the use of habit evidence in criminal cases only in the narrow circumstances of *Graham*, as construed in *Ligon*"). Thus Rule 2:406 neither prohibits nor enables the use of habit evidence in criminal cases, although *Ligon* and character evidence rules present serious obstacles to its admission.

FED. R. EV. 407. SUBSEQUENT REMEDIAL MEASURES

When measures are taken that would have made an earlier injury or harm less likely to occur, evidence of the subsequent measures is not admissible to prove:

- negligence;

- culpable conduct;

- a defect in a product or its design; or

- a need for a warning or instruction.

But the court may admit this evidence for another purpose, such as impeachment or--if disputed--proving ownership, control, or the feasibility of precautionary measures.

VA. R. EV. 2:407. SUBSEQUENT REMEDIAL MEASURES (derived from Code § 8.01-418.1)

When, after the occurrence of an event, measures are taken which, if taken prior to the event, would have made the event less likely to occur, evidence of such subsequent measures is not admissible to prove negligence or culpable conduct as a cause of the occurrence of the event; provided that evidence of subsequent measures shall not be required to be excluded when offered for another purpose for which it may be admissible, including, but not limited to, proof of ownership, control, feasibility of precautionary measures if controverted, or for impeachment.

Comparison and Commentary

The federal and Virginia rules generally bar admission of subsequent remedial measures. The respective rules are largely based on the policy rationale that permitting such evidence creates a disincentive to mitigate dangerous conditions. Turner v. Manning, Maxwell & Moore, Inc., 216 Va. 245, 253, 217 S.E.2d 863, 869 (Va. 1975) (discussing "public policy underlying the rule"). The Virginia rule comes from a 1978 statute, Va. Code § 8.01-418.1. That statute generally tracks the language of the original Federal Rule 407. As the Federal Rule has been amended twice since its original enactment to clarify ambiguities, the Virginia rule continues to incorporate three ambiguities that have been ironed out of its federal cousin.

First, the Virginia rule uses "occurrence of an event" to describe the operative litigation-generating incident, but this phrasing is vague. The federal rule added "injury or harm allegedly caused by an event" in 1997 to "clarify that the rule applies only to [remedial measures] made after the occurrence that produced the damages giving rise to the [instant] action." Advisory Committee Note to 1997 Amendment; but see Raymond v. Raymond Corp., 938 F.2d 1518, 1523 (1st Cir. 1991) (recognizing even before amendment that "[t]he term 'event' refers to the accident that precipitated the suit"). The sparse Virginia case law on the topic does not address the issue.

Second, the text of the Virginia rule does not clearly indicate whether the "if controverted" qualification applies solely to the "feasibility of precautionary measures" or also to the earlier-listed permitted uses (e.g., ownership and control). Again, Virginia case law does not resolve the question. The restyling of the federal rules in 2011 clarified that the qualifier (recast as "if disputed") applies to feasibility, ownership and control.

Third, in 1997, the federal rule was "amended to provide that evidence of subsequent remedial measures may not be used to prove 'a defect in a product or its design, or that a warning or instruction should have accompanied a product.'" Advisory Committee Note to 1997 Amendment. As this language has not been added to the Virginia rule, the Virginia rule's applicability in products liability cases might seem unclear. Indeed, the Virginia codifiers make this point explicit, stating: "This statute takes no position on product liability cases." Codification Commentary to Rule 2:407. (The Commentary cites Gordon Harper Harley-Davidson Sales, Inc. v. Cutchin, 232 Va. 320, 325, 350 S.E.2d 609, 612 (Va. 1986), a case which includes no reference to the remedial measures bar in affirming admission of a service bulletin objected to, in part, "on public-policy grounds.") In truth, however, there should be no question regarding the applicability of the statute to Virginia products liability cases (and the *Gordon* case cited by the codifiers probably just failed to realize the statute's potential applicability). The pre-amendment federal ambiguity arose because Rule 407 did not seem to apply where the substantive standard was "strict liability" (as opposed to negligence), and products liability actions in federal court were often governed by a strict liability standard. See Robbins v. Farmers Union Grain Terminal Ass'n, 552 F.2d 788, 793 (8th Cir. 1977) ("Rule 407 is, by its terms, confined to cases involving negligence or other culpable conduct. The doctrine of strict liability by its very nature, does not include these elements."). Virginia does not recognize strict liability in products liability cases. See Sensenbrenner v. Rust, Orling & Neale, Architects, Inc., 236 Va. 419, 424 n.4, 374 S.E.2d 55, 57 n.4 (Va. 1988) ("Virginia law has not adopted § 402A of the Restatement (Second) of Torts and does not permit tort recovery on a strict-liability theory in products-liability cases.") Consequently, there should be no ambiguity about Rule 2:407's application to Virginia products liability cases, which are simply "negligence or culpable conduct" cases to which the rule by its terms applies. Ambiguity remains, of course, in Virginia cases premised on strict liability causes of action, but this is a narrow set of "ultrahazardous" activities in Virginia. See, e.g., M. W. Worley Const. v. Hungerford, Inc., 215 Va. 377, 381, 210 S.E.2d 161, 164 (Va. 1974) ("blasting").

FED. R. EV. 408. COMPROMISE OFFERS AND NEGOTIATIONS

(a) Prohibited Uses. Evidence of the following is not admissible--on behalf of any party--either to prove or disprove the validity or amount of a disputed claim or to impeach by a prior inconsistent statement or a contradiction:

> **(1)** furnishing, promising, or offering--or accepting, promising to accept, or offering to accept--a valuable consideration in compromising or attempting to compromise the claim; and

> **(2)** conduct or a statement made during compromise negotiations about the claim--except when offered in a criminal case and when the negotiations related to a claim by a public office in the exercise of its regulatory, investigative, or enforcement authority.

(b) Exceptions. The court may admit this evidence for another purpose, such as proving a witness's bias or prejudice, negating a contention of undue delay, or proving an effort to obstruct a criminal investigation or prosecution.

VA. R. EV. 2:408. COMPROMISE AND OFFERS TO COMPROMISE

Evidence of offers and responses concerning settlement or compromise of any claim which is disputed as to liability or amount is inadmissible regarding such issues. However, an express admission of liability, or an admission concerning an independent fact pertinent to a question in issue, is admissible even if made during settlement negotiations. Otherwise admissible evidence is not excludable merely because it was presented in the course of compromise negotiations. Nor is it required that evidence of settlement or compromise negotiations be excluded if the evidence is offered for another purpose, such as proving bias or prejudice of a witness or negating a contention of undue delay.

Comparison and Commentary

The Virginia and federal rules forbid the introduction of certain evidence regarding settlement negotiations. Both rules prohibit offers to settle if tendered to prove the validity or amount of a disputed claim. The Virginia rule is clearer that "responses thereto" are also covered; the federal rule implicitly covers such responses. Both rules are based on the public policy of promoting compromise.

The primary distinction between the two rules is that the federal rule also renders inadmissible any statement made during settlement discussions. Virginia, by contrast, provides no protection for an "express admission of liability, or an admission concerning an independent fact pertinent to a question in issue."

The Virginia rule comes straight from case law, although that case law is conclusory and provides little exposition. See Lyle, Siegel, Croshaw & Beale, P.C. v. Tidewater Capital Corp., 249 Va. 426, 438, 457 S.E.2d 28, 35 (Va. 1995) (stating general rule, but highlighting precedent for proposition that "an admission during settlement negotiations of an independent fact pertinent to a question in issue" and "an express admission of liability made during settlement negotiations" are admissible). The Virginia rule is best understood by tracing its origins to the general common-law rule that permitted the introduction at trial of "admissions of fact" even if made during settlement negotiations. This common-law rule is specifically disparaged in the federal advisory committee notes. See Advisory Committee Note to Fed. R. Evid. 408 (indicating departure from common-law rule's "inapplicability to admissions of fact, even though made in the course of compromise negotiations, unless hypothetical, stated to be 'without prejudice,' or so connected with the offer as to be inseparable from it"). Given this pedigree, it becomes clear that the "independent" facts referred to in the Virginia rule are simply facts stated without qualifying language (e.g., "without prejudice") and not otherwise directly tethered to the offer of compromise. See Hendrickson v. Meredith, 161 Va. 193, 204, 170 S.E. 602, 606 (Va. 1933) (quoting following discussion with approval: "confidential overtures of pacification, and any other offers or propositions between litigating parties, expressly stated to be made without prejudice, are excluded on grounds of public policy. *** But if it is an independent admission of a fact, merely because it is a fact, it will be received; and even the offer of a sum by way of compromise of a claim tacitly admitted is receivable, unless accompanied with a caution that the offer is confidential.'") Thus, a pertinent fact uttered during settlement discussions that is not carefully couched in qualifying language is potentially admissible under Rule 2:408.

The Virginia rule also carves out "explicit admission[s] of liability" from its protection. The meaning here is more obscure, but best understood as simply a particularly damaging subset of "independent" fact admissions. See City of Richmond v. A. H. Ewing's Sons, 201 Va. 862, 869-70, 114 S.E.2d 608, 613 (Va. 1960) ("The recognition of the existence of a binding contract was in the nature of an admission of an independent fact pertinent to the issue of the correctness of the claims.... Upon this principle an express admission of liability made during negotiations for a compromise is admissible.") Just as a statement of fact uttered during settlement negotiations will be admissible under the Virginia rule, so will an "explicit admission of liability" unless the admission is explicitly qualified or shown from the circumstances to be an integral part of the compromise offer itself.

The Virginia rule does not capture two changes made to the federal rule in a 2006 amendment. Most importantly, the 2006 amendment explicitly prohibits the use of settlement statements for "impeach[ment]." Fed. R. Evid. 408(a); Advisory Committee Note to 2006 Amendment ("The amendment prohibits the use of statements made in settlement negotiations when offered to impeach by prior inconsistent statement or through contradiction. Such broad impeachment would tend to swallow the exclusionary rule and would impair the public policy of promoting settlements.") In Virginia, the rule is otherwise. See Codification Commentary to Rule 2:408 ("Virginia law allows evidence relating to a compromise to be admitted for purposes other than concession of liability, such as to contradict a witness.") (citing Fielding v. Robertson, 141 Va. 123, 138, 126 S.E. 231, 236 (Va. 1925) (rejecting challenge to evidence about compromise negotiation where "the question put to Fielding was not to show an unaccepted offer of compromise, but to ... contradict the statement of Fielding")).

Second, the 2006 amendment provides an exception to the federal rule's protections for certain statements made during compromise negotiations with a government agency. Fed. R. Ev. 408(a)(2). Virginia's rule contains no such provision.

FED. R. EV. 409. OFFERS TO PAY MEDICAL AND SIMILAR EXPENSES

Evidence of furnishing, promising to pay, or offering to pay medical, hospital, or similar expenses resulting from an injury is not admissible to prove liability for the injury.

[ed.-- Virginia Rule 2:409 (see below) covers a different subject than Fed. R. Ev. 409. More closely analogous to Fed. R. Ev. 409 are two Virginia statutes covering expressions of sympathy, reprinted below.]

VA. CODE §§ 8.01-52.1 AND 8.01-581.20:1. ADMISSIBILITY OF EXPRESSIONS OF SYMPATHY

In any wrongful death action brought pursuant to §8.01-50 against a health care provider, or in any arbitration or medical malpractice review panel proceeding related to such wrongful death action, [§ 8.01-52.1]

In any civil action brought by an alleged victim of an unanticipated outcome of health care, or in any arbitration or medical malpractice review panel proceeding related to such civil action, [§8.01-581.20:1],

the portion of statements, writings, affirmations, benevolent conduct, or benevolent gestures expressing sympathy, commiseration, condolence, compassion, or a general sense of benevolence, together with apologies that are made by a health care provider or an agent of a health care provider to a relative of the patient, or a representative of the patient ["about the death of the patient as a result of the unanticipated outcome of health care," – §8.01-52.1 only] shall be inadmissible as evidence of an admission of liability or as evidence of an admission against interest. A statement of fault that is part of or in addition to any of the above shall not be made inadmissible by this section....

[ed. – definition section omitted]

Comparison and Commentary

The federal evidence code bars evidence of offers to pay medical expenses when offered to prove liability for an injury. The provision is designed to reduce disincentives to such benevolent gestures. Neither the Virginia codification nor its case law includes a similar provision. Presumably, then, such offers are admissible in Virginia courts to prove liability through a consciousness of guilt theory.

Virginia does have two narrow "apology" evidence statutes designed to limit the admissibility of expressions of sympathy, reprinted above. The statutes only apply in civil actions against health care providers, and both create exceptions that allow parties to offer "statement[s] of fault," dramatically limiting the significance of these statutes. See Jonathan R. Cohen, *Legislating Apology: The Pros and Cons*, 70 U. Cin. L.

Rev. 819, 831 (2002) (discussing legislative movement to exclude apologies, but noting that statutes that retain admissibility of statements of fault represent only minor changes from the status quo because "a statement which merely expresses sympathy or benevolence after an injury has little probative value on the issue of fault"). The Virginia statutes are tailored to different actions (wrongful death occasioned by medical negligence and medical malpractice more generally), but are otherwise identical. There is no equivalent federal protection against the use of apologies as evidence at trial.

VA. R. EV. 2:409. EVIDENCE OF ABUSE ADMISSIBLE IN CERTAIN CRIMINAL TRIALS (derived from Code § 19.2-270.6)

In any criminal prosecution alleging personal injury or death, or the attempt to cause personal injury or death, relevant evidence of repeated physical and psychological abuse of the accused by the victim shall be admissible, subject to the general rules of evidence.

Comparison and Commentary

Virginia has a rule specifically addressing evidence of abuse of the accused by the victim. The 1993 statute from which the rule is derived seems directed toward evidence supporting a defense based on "battered woman's syndrome" (minus the requisite expert). The statute does not appear in any published Virginia opinion. It is unclear what the statute (and thus Rule) accomplishes, other than stating a non-binding legislative endorsement of such evidence, since it explicitly states that any evidence falling within the rule must also survive the "general rules of evidence."

FED. R. EV. 410. PLEAS, PLEA DISCUSSIONS, AND RELATED STATEMENTS

(a) Prohibited Uses. In a civil or criminal case, evidence of the following is not admissible against the defendant who made the plea or participated in the plea discussions:

(1) a guilty plea that was later withdrawn;

(2) a nolo contendere plea;

(3) a statement made during a proceeding on either of those pleas under Federal Rule of Criminal Procedure 11 or a comparable state procedure; or

(4) a statement made during plea discussions with an attorney for the prosecuting authority if the discussions did not result in a guilty plea or they resulted in a later-withdrawn guilty plea.

(b) Exceptions. The court may admit a statement described in Rule 410(a)(3) or (4):

(1) in any proceeding in which another statement made during the same plea or plea discussions has been introduced, if in fairness the statements ought to be considered together; or

(2) in a criminal proceeding for perjury or false statement, if the defendant made the statement under oath, on the record, and with counsel present.

VA. R. EV. 2:410. WITHDRAWN PLEAS, OFFERS TO PLEAD, AND RELATED STATEMENTS

Admission of evidence concerning withdrawn pleas in criminal cases, offers to plead, and related statements shall be governed by Rule 3A:8(c)(5) of the Rules of Supreme Court of Virginia and by applicable provisions of the Code of Virginia.

VA. SUP. CT. R. 3A:8. PLEAS

... (c)(5) Except as otherwise provided by law, evidence of a plea of guilty later withdrawn, or a plea of nolo contendere, or of an offer to plead guilty or nolo contendere to the crime charged, or any other crime, or of statements made in connection with and relevant to any of the foregoing pleas or offers, is not admissible in the case-in-chief in any civil or criminal proceeding against the person who made the plea or offer. But evidence of a statement made in connection with and relevant to a plea of guilty, later withdrawn, a plea of nolo contendere, or any offer to plead guilty or nolo contendere to the crime charged or to any other crime, is admissible in any criminal proceeding for perjury or false statement, if the statement was made by the defendant under oath and on the record....

Comparison and Commentary

The Virginia and federal rules shield guilty plea negotiations from admissibility in a later proceeding. The respective rules use of similar language masks significant distinctions.

First, the Virginia rule differs dramatically from its federal counterpart by limiting its scope to the prosecution's (or civil party's) case-in-chief. This limitation is significant. Under the Virginia rule, a defendant can be impeached on cross-examination with statements made during guilty plea negotiations. The prosecution may also introduce evidence from unsuccessful plea negotiations in its rebuttal case. See Com. v. Evans, 55 Va. Cir. 237 (Va. Cir. 2001) ("Unlike the parallel federal rules, the plain meaning of Rule 3A:8(c)(5) only precludes the admission of the statement in the "case-in-chief" against the defendant at trial. Thus, the prosecution may use the statement against the defendant as impeachment on cross-examination or during the rebuttal phase of the trial.") A similar result can be obtained in the federal system only through waivers requested as a condition of initiating plea negotiations. See United States v. Mezzanatto, 513 U.S. 196, 210 (1995) (rejecting challenge to waiver of Rule 410's impeachment prohibition).

Another notable textual distinction is that the Virginia rule does not include the qualifier, present in the federal rule, that covered statements must be made in the course of plea discussions "with an attorney for the prosecuting attorney." The qualifier was added to the federal rule by a 1980 amendment designed to remove "confrontations between suspects and law enforcement agents" from the scope of the rule and eliminate the prospect that "an otherwise voluntary admission to law enforcement officials is rendered inadmissible merely because it was made in the hope of obtaining leniency by a plea." Federal Advisory Committee Note to 1980 Amendment. As Virginia did not incorporate that change in its rule, the implication remains that a defendant's statement to an arresting police officer, "I want to plead guilty, I committed the crime," is properly excluded under Rule 2:410.

Virginia's rule does not include the "rule of completeness" provision included in Federal Rule 410(b)(1) and, as noted earlier, Virginia's own "rule of completeness," Rule 2:106, may not provide the same level of assistance as Rule 410(b)(1).

Virginia's rule also more clearly extends to prohibit evidence that the prosecution offered a plea, by excluding any offer "against the person who made the plea or offer." The federal rule by contrast only applies, by its terms, when evidence of a plea is offered "against the defendant." See U.S. v. Biaggi, 909 F.2d 662, 690 (2d Cir. 1990) ("Preliminarily, we note that plea negotiations are inadmissible 'against the defendant,' Fed.R.Crim.P. 11(e)(6); Fed.R.Evid. 410, and it does not necessarily follow that the Government is entitled to a similar shield."). Still, there is support even in the federal system for excluding plea offers made by the government. See Advisory Committee Note to 1980 Amendment ("no disapproval is intended of such decisions as United States v. Verdoorn, 528 F.2d 103 (8th Cir. 1976), holding that the trial judge properly refused to permit the defendants to put into evidence at their trial the fact [that] the prosecution had attempted to plea bargain with them ....")

Virginia Code § 8.01-418 permits introduction of a party's completed guilty plea or plea of nolo contendere in a civil action arising out of the same occurrence. This provision does not extend to guilty or nolo pleas of non-parties. Ayala v. Aggressive Towing & Transp., 276 Va. 169, 174, 661 S.E.2d 480, 482 (2008). The statute's treatment of nolo contendere pleas is different from that in Federal Rule 410 and appears inconsistent with the explicit exclusion of nolo contendere pleas in Virginia Supreme Court Rule 3A:8 (reprinted above).

FED. R. EV. 411. LIABILITY INSURANCE

Evidence that a person was or was not insured against liability is not admissible to prove whether the person acted negligently or otherwise wrongfully. But the court may admit this evidence for another purpose, such as proving a witness's bias or prejudice or proving agency, ownership, or control.

VA. R. EV. 2:411. INSURANCE

Evidence that a person was or was not insured is not admissible on the question whether the person acted negligently or otherwise wrongfully, and not admissible on the issue of damages. But exclusion of evidence of insurance is not required when offered for another purpose, such as proof of agency, ownership, or control, or bias or prejudice of a witness.

Comparison and Commentary

Using similar language, the Virginia and federal rules prohibit evidence of insurance coverage offered to prove culpability. As with federal case law, Virginia case law on these questions is sparse. The most thorough articulation of the governing law in Virginia mirrors the federal rule:

> "We reaffirm the general principle that evidence as to whether a defendant did or did not carry liability insurance is generally irrelevant and inadmissible in a trial to address issues of negligence, causation, and damages. However, consistent with our prior cases and the majority view in the United States, we hold that testimony concerning liability insurance may be elicited for the purpose of showing bias or prejudice of a witness if there is a substantial connection between the witness and the liability carrier." Lombard v. Rohrbaugh, 262 Va. 484, 497, 551 S.E.2d 349, 356 (Va. 2001).

The two textual distinctions between the federal and Virginia rule speak more to drafting preferences than substantive differences. First, the federal rule only addresses insurance "against liability" (a qualifier omitted in the Virginia rule). As the Virginia rule makes clear, a prohibition of evidence of insurance should logically apply beyond "liability" insurance to other forms of insurance such as life or health insurance. The danger of the factfinder's assigning fault to the party who can most easily bear the cost (rather than the party legally at fault) applies regardless of the type of insurance available to compensate the injured party. A jury learning about applicable health and life insurance, for example, could be just as unfairly prejudiced as one hearing about "liability" insurance. Thus, Rule 411 should logically extend to all forms of insurance. In the federal rules' drafters defense, however, it is difficult to imagine situations where evidence of health or life insurance could be relevant to establish liability or culpable conduct, so Rule 411's extension to these forms of insurance seems almost as unnecessary as it is logical.

Second, the Virginia rule adds that evidence of insurance is also not admissible "on the issue of damages" (omitted from the federal rule). It is fairly uncontroversial that a prohibition of evidence of insurance coverage should also extend to efforts to use such coverage to influence a jury's calculation of damages. Thus, the Virginia rule's explicit inclusion of such efforts in the rule's prohibition is understandable. Again, however, it is difficult to see how evidence of insurance coverage could be legally relevant to damages in jurisdictions that exclude insurance coverage from damage calculations.

FED. R. EV. 412. SEX-OFFENSE CASES: THE VICTIM'S SEXUAL BEHAVIOR OR PREDISPOSITION

(a) Prohibited Uses. The following evidence is not admissible in a civil or criminal proceeding involving alleged sexual misconduct:

> **(1)** evidence offered to prove that a victim engaged in other sexual behavior; or
>
> **(2)** evidence offered to prove a victim's sexual predisposition.

(b) Exceptions.

> **(1) Criminal Cases.** The court may admit the following evidence in a criminal case:
>
>> **(A)** evidence of specific instances of a victim's sexual behavior, if offered to prove that someone other than the defendant was the source of semen, injury, or other physical evidence;
>>
>> **(B)** evidence of specific instances of a victim's sexual behavior with respect to the person accused of the sexual misconduct, if offered by the defendant to prove consent or if offered by the prosecutor; and

(C) evidence whose exclusion would violate the defendant's constitutional rights.

(2) Civil Cases. In a civil case, the court may admit evidence offered to prove a victim's sexual behavior or sexual predisposition if its probative value substantially outweighs the danger of harm to any victim and of unfair prejudice to any party. The court may admit evidence of a victim's reputation only if the victim has placed it in controversy.

(c) Procedure to Determine Admissibility.

(1) Motion. If a party intends to offer evidence under Rule 412(b), the party must:

(A) file a motion that specifically describes the evidence and states the purpose for which it is to be offered;

(B) do so at least 14 days before trial unless the court, for good cause, sets a different time;

(C) serve the motion on all parties; and

(D) notify the victim or, when appropriate, the victim's guardian or representative.

(2) Hearing. Before admitting evidence under this rule, the court must conduct an in camera hearing and give the victim and parties a right to attend and be heard. Unless the court orders otherwise, the motion, related materials, and the record of the hearing must be and remain sealed.

(d) Definition of "Victim." In this rule, "victim" includes an alleged victim.

VA. R. EV. 2:412. ADMISSIBILITY OF COMPLAINING WITNESS' PRIOR SEXUAL CONDUCT; CRIMINAL SEXUAL ASSAULT CASES; RELEVANCE OF PAST BEHAVIOR (derived from Code § 18.2-67.7)

(a) In prosecutions under Article 7, Chapter 4 of Title 18.2 of the Code of Virginia [ed.-- sexual assault], under clause (iii) or (iv) of § 18.2-48 [ed.-- abduction for prostitution], or under §§ 18.2-370, 18.2-370.01, or 18.2-370.1 [ed.-- indecent liberties with a child], general reputation or opinion evidence of the complaining witness' unchaste character or prior sexual conduct shall not be admitted. Unless the complaining witness voluntarily agrees otherwise, evidence of specific instances of his or her prior sexual conduct shall be admitted only if it is relevant and is:

1. Evidence offered to provide an alternative explanation for physical evidence of the offense charged which is introduced by the prosecution, limited to evidence designed to explain the presence of semen, pregnancy, disease, or physical injury to the complaining witness' intimate parts; or

2. Evidence of sexual conduct between the complaining witness and the accused offered to support a contention that the alleged offense was not accomplished by force, threat or intimidation or through the use of the complaining witness' mental incapacity or physical helplessness, provided that the sexual conduct occurred within a period of time reasonably proximate to the offense charged under the circumstances of this case; or

3. Evidence offered to rebut evidence of the complaining witness' prior sexual conduct introduced by the prosecution.

(b) Nothing contained in this Rule shall prohibit the accused from presenting evidence relevant to show that the complaining witness had a motive to fabricate the charge against the accused. If such evidence relates to the past sexual conduct of the complaining witness with a person other than the accused, it shall not be admitted and may not be referred to at any preliminary hearing or trial unless the party offering same files a written notice generally describing the evidence prior to the introduction of any evidence, or the opening statement of either counsel, whichever first occurs, at the preliminary hearing or trial at which the admission of the evidence may be sought.

(c) Evidence described in subdivisions (a) and (b) of this Rule shall not be admitted and may not be referred to at any preliminary hearing or trial until the court first determines the admissibility of that evidence at an evidentiary hearing to be held before the evidence is introduced at such preliminary hearing or trial. The court shall exclude from the evidentiary hearing all persons except the accused, the complaining witness, other necessary witnesses, and required court personnel. If the court determines that the evidence meets the requirements of subdivisions (a) and (b) of this Rule, it shall be admissible before the judge or jury trying the case in the ordinary course of the preliminary hearing or trial. If the court initially determines that the evidence is inadmissible, but new information is discovered during the course of the preliminary hearing or trial which may make such evidence admissible, the court shall determine in an evidentiary hearing whether such evidence is admissible.

Comparison and Commentary

Both the federal and Virginia rules include a "Rape Shield" provision designed to exclude evidence of victims' past sexual conduct offered by defendants as impeachment or to suggest consent. Both rules generally bar opinion or reputation evidence, along with evidence of specific conduct relating to a victim's sexual behavior or disposition.

The Virginia rule tracks the federal rule prior to its amendment in 1994. The post-amendment federal rule applies in any civil or criminal proceeding "involving alleged sexual misconduct"; this includes cases where there is no formal charge or allegation of a sex-related offense. The Virginia rule, by contrast, only applies in cases involving the enumerated sexual-offense-related charges and has no application in civil cases.

Both rules contain two similar exceptions: evidence of a victim's past sexual conduct is permitted to explain physical evidence; or to suggest consent if the past sexual conduct was with the accused. The Virginia rule includes a provision not contained in the federal rule that allows the defense to rebut evidence offered by the prosecution. This provision is likely included to account for another distinction in the Virginia rule which allows for introduction of specific instances of the victim's prior sexual conduct if "the complaining witness voluntarily agrees" to their admission. If the prosecution takes advantage of this provision, Rule 2:412(a)(3) allows the defense to rebut the prosecution evidence.

The Virginia rule includes a provision ensuring that the accused can present evidence relevant to show a "complaining witness's motive to fabricate the charge against the accused." No such provision is included in the federal rule, although scenarios that implicate this Virginia provision will often trigger the constitutional requirement for admission of significant, exonerating evidence referenced in Federal Rule 412(b)(1)(C). See Olden v. Kentucky, 488 U.S. 227, 232 (1988).

As noted, the federal rule contains an explicit exception for evidence whose exclusion would violate the defendant's constitutional rights. This provision is unnecessary since the Constitution trumps the evidence code with or without the code's permission and is understandably omitted from the Virginia rule.

Both rules require a hearing intended to protect the victim's privacy interests prior to admission of evidence implicating this rule.

RULES 413-415, EDITOR'S INTRODUCTORY NOTE

Congress added Federal Rules 413-415 in 1995 to strengthen prosecutions and civil actions against recidivist sex offenders. The only Virginia analogue to these rules is Rule 2:413 adopted in 2014. Rule 2:413 most closely parallels Federal Rule 414. Each of the rules is set forth below, prior to a Comparison and Commentary Section that addresses them all.

FED. R. EV. 413. SIMILAR CRIMES IN SEXUAL-ASSAULT CASES

(a) Permitted Uses. In a criminal case in which a defendant is accused of a sexual assault, the court may admit evidence that the defendant committed any other sexual assault. The evidence may be considered on any matter to which it is relevant.

(b) Disclosure to the Defendant. If the prosecutor intends to offer this evidence, the prosecutor must disclose it to the defendant, including witnesses' statements or a summary of the expected testimony. The prosecutor must do so at least 15 days before trial or at a later time that the court allows for good cause.

(c) Effect on Other Rules. This rule does not limit the admission or consideration of evidence under any other rule.

(d) Definition of "Sexual Assault." In this rule and Rule 415, " sexual assault" means a crime under federal law or under state law (as " state" is defined in 18 U.S.C. § 513) involving:

(1) any conduct prohibited by 18 U.S.C. chapter 109A;

(2) contact, without consent, between any part of the defendant's body--or an object--and another person's genitals or anus;

(3) contact, without consent, between the defendant's genitals or anus and any part of another person's body;

(4) deriving sexual pleasure or gratification from inflicting death, bodily injury, or physical pain on another person; or

(5) an attempt or conspiracy to engage in conduct described in subparagraphs (1)-(4).

VA. R. EV. 2:413. EVIDENCE OF SIMILAR CRIMES IN CHILD SEXUAL OFFENSE CASES (derived from Code § 18.2-67.7:1)

(a) In a criminal case in which the defendant is accused of a felony sexual offense involving a child victim, evidence of the defendant's conviction of another sexual offense or offenses is admissible and may be considered for its bearing on any matter to which it is relevant.

(b) The Commonwealth shall provide to the defendant 14 days prior to trial notice of its intention to introduce copies of final orders evidencing the defendant's qualifying prior criminal convictions. Such notice shall include (i) the date of each prior conviction, (ii) the name and jurisdiction of the court where each prior conviction was obtained, and (iii) each offense of which the defendant was convicted. Prior to commencement of the trial, the Commonwealth shall provide to the defendant photocopies of certified copies of the final orders that it intends to introduce.

(c) This Rule shall not be construed to limit the admission or consideration of evidence under any other section or rule of court.

(d) For purposes of this Rule, "sexual offense" means any offense or any attempt or conspiracy to engage in any offense described in Article 7 (§ 18.2-61 et seq.) of Chapter 4 or § 18.2-370, 18.2-370.01, or 18.2-370.1 or any substantially similar offense under the laws of another state or territory of the United States, the District of Columbia, or the United States.

(e) Evidence offered in a criminal case pursuant to the provisions of this section shall be subject to exclusion in accordance with the Virginia Rules of Evidence, including but not limited to Rule 2:403.

FED. R. EV. 414. SIMILAR CRIMES IN CHILD-MOLESTATION CASES

(a) Permitted Uses. In a criminal case in which a defendant is accused of child molestation, the court may admit evidence that the defendant committed any other child molestation. The evidence may be considered on any matter to which it is relevant.

(b) Disclosure to the Defendant. If the prosecutor intends to offer this evidence, the prosecutor must disclose it to the defendant, including witnesses' statements or a summary of the expected testimony. The prosecutor must do so at least 15 days before trial or at a later time that the court allows for good cause.

(c) Effect on Other Rules. This rule does not limit the admission or consideration of evidence under any other rule.

(d) Definition of "Child" and "Child Molestation." In this rule and Rule 415:

(1) "child" means a person below the age of 14; and

(2) "child molestation" means a crime under federal law or

under state law (as "state" is defined in 18 U.S.C. § 513) involving:

(A) any conduct prohibited by 18 U.S.C. chapter 109A and committed with a child;

(B) any conduct prohibited by 18 U.S.C. chapter 110;

(C) contact between any part of the defendant's body-- or an object--and a child's genitals or anus;

(D) contact between the defendant's genitals or anus and any part of a child's body;

(E) deriving sexual pleasure or gratification from inflicting death, bodily injury, or physical pain on a child; or

(F) an attempt or conspiracy to engage in conduct described in subparagraphs (A)-(E).

FED. R. EV. 415. SIMILAR ACTS IN CIVIL CASES INVOLVING SEXUAL ASSAULT OR CHILD MOLESTATION

(a) **Permitted Uses.** In a civil case involving a claim for relief based on a party's alleged sexual assault or child molestation, the court may admit evidence that the party committed any other sexual assault or child molestation. The evidence may be considered as provided in Rules 413 and 414.

(b) **Disclosure to the Opponent.** If a party intends to offer this evidence, the party must disclose it to the party against whom it will be offered, including witnesses' statements or a summary of the expected testimony. The party must do so at least 15 days before trial or at a later time that the court allows for good cause.

(c) Effect on Other Rules. This rule does not limit the admission or consideration of evidence under any other rule.

Comparison and Commentary

The federal rules create an exception to the propensity ban in Rule 404 for uncharged acts of sexual assault in sexual assault prosecutions, uncharged acts of child molestation in child molestation prosecutions, and other acts of either type in parallel civil suits. Virginia's rules include an analogue to only one of the federal rules – the rule for child sexual offense cases, labeled Rule 2:413, added in 2014. The federal analogue is Rule 414. There is no Virginia analogue to Rule 413 or Rule 415.

Virginia's Rule 2:413 is distinct from Federal Rule 414 in significant respects. First, the Virginia rule only permits the use of prior "conviction[s]," while the federal rule permits any relevant "evidence of child molestation." This significantly narrows the scope of evidence admissible under the Virginia rule. Second, the Virginia rule permits any conviction of any "sexual offense," cross-referencing in the definition of that term sexual offenses such as rape (§18.2-61) that do not necessarily involve minors. (The federal rule, by contrast, only permits evidence of sexual offenses committed against a "child," defined in that rule as a person "below the age of 14.") Whether a sexual crime committed against an adult victim will be deemed "relevant" to show a defendant's propensity to assault a child has yet to be determined by the Virginia courts. If the answer is yes, than this federal-state distinction will be a meaningful one. Third, the Virginia rule only applies in felony prosecutions, while the federal analogue is not explicitly limited to any subset of prosecutions.

Both rules contain similar notice provisions. Rule 2:413(e) states that evidence falling under the Rule may still be excluded by Rule 2:403. This is the same conclusion reached through case law in the federal courts, despite the absence of such a provision in Rules 413-415 and arguably contrary language in the federal rules' pre-restyled text.

Virginia's proviso that evidence admissible under Rule 2:413 could be excluded by the other evidence rules seems to set up a clash with Rule 2:404, but Rule 2:404(b) was amended to include an express exception for Rule 2:413, conforming the two rules.

Given the very recent enactment of Rule 2:413, there is no pertinent case law involving the rule.

ARTICLE V. PRIVILEGES

FED. R. EV. 501. PRIVILEGE IN GENERAL

The common law--as interpreted by United States courts in the light of reason and experience--governs a claim of privilege unless any of the following provides otherwise:

- the United States Constitution;

- a federal statute; or

- rules prescribed by the Supreme Court.

But in a civil case, state law governs privilege regarding a claim or defense for which state law supplies the rule of decision.

VA. R. EV. 2:501. PRIVILEGED COMMUNICATIONS

Except as otherwise required by the Constitutions of the United States or the Commonwealth of Virginia or provided by statute or these Rules, the privilege of a witness, person, government, State, or political subdivision thereof, shall be governed by the principles of common law as they may be interpreted by the courts of the Commonwealth in the light of reason and experience.

Comparison and Commentary

The federal and Virginia rules both contain a rule deferring development of privilege rules to the courts. The federal rules further defer to state privilege law when state law provides the rule of decision. Unlike the federal evidence code, however, the Virginia rules include Rules 2:503-507, discussed below, that delineate Virginia's primarily statute-based privilege law.

FED. R. EV. 502. ATTORNEY-CLIENT PRIVILEGE AND WORK PRODUCT; LIMITATIONS ON WAIVER

The following provisions apply, in the circumstances set out, to disclosure of a communication or information covered by the attorney-client privilege or work-product protection.

(a) Disclosure Made in a Federal Proceeding or to a Federal Office or Agency; Scope of a Waiver. When the disclosure is made in a federal proceeding or to a federal office or agency and waives the attorney-client privilege or work-product protection, the waiver extends to an undisclosed communication or information in a federal or state proceeding only if:

(1) the waiver is intentional;

(2) the disclosed and undisclosed communications or information concern the same subject matter; and

(3) they ought in fairness to be considered together.

(b) Inadvertent Disclosure. When made in a federal proceeding or to a federal office or agency, the disclosure does not operate as a waiver in a federal or state proceeding if:

(1) the disclosure is inadvertent;

(2) the holder of the privilege or protection took reasonable steps to prevent disclosure; and

(3) the holder promptly took reasonable steps to rectify the error, including (if applicable) following Federal Rule of Civil Procedure 26(b)(5)(B).

(c) Disclosure Made in a State Proceeding. When the disclosure is made in a state proceeding and is not the subject of a state-court order concerning waiver, the disclosure does not operate as a waiver in a federal proceeding if the disclosure:

(1) would not be a waiver under this rule if it had been made in a federal proceeding; or

(2) is not a waiver under the law of the state where the disclosure occurred.

(d) Controlling Effect of a Court Order. A federal court may order that the privilege or protection is not waived by disclosure connected with the litigation pending before the court--in which event the disclosure is also not a waiver in any other federal or state proceeding.

(e) Controlling Effect of a Party Agreement. An agreement on the effect of disclosure in a federal proceeding is binding only on the parties to the agreement, unless it is incorporated into a court order.

(f) Controlling Effect of This Rule. Notwithstanding Rules 101 and 1101, this rule applies to state proceedings and to federal court-annexed and federal court-mandated arbitration proceedings, in the circumstances set out in the rule. And notwithstanding Rule 501, this rule applies even if state law provides the rule of decision.

(g) Definitions. In this rule:

(1) "attorney-client privilege" means the protection that applicable law provides for confidential attorney-client communications; and

(2) "work-product protection" means the protection that applicable law provides for tangible material (or its intangible equivalent) prepared in anticipation of litigation or for trial.

VA. CODE § 8.01-420.7. ATTORNEY-CLIENT PRIVILEGE AND WORK PRODUCT PROTECTION; LIMITATIONS ON WAIVER

A. When disclosure of a communication or information covered by the attorney-client privilege or work product protection made in a proceeding or to any public body as defined in § 2.2-3701 operates as a waiver of the privilege or protection, the waiver extends to an undisclosed communication or information only if:

> 1. The waiver is intentional;

> 2. The disclosed and undisclosed communications or information concern the same subject matter; and

> 3. The disclosed and undisclosed communications or information ought in fairness be considered together.

B. Disclosure of a communication or information covered by the attorney-client privilege or work product protection made in a proceeding or to any public body as defined in § 2.2-3701 does not operate as a waiver of the privilege or protection if:

> 1. The disclosure is inadvertent;

> 2. The holder of the privilege or protection took reasonable steps to prevent disclosure; and

> 3. The holder promptly took reasonable steps to rectify the error, including, if applicable, complying with the provisions of subdivision (b)(6)(ii) of Rule 4:1 of the Rules of the Supreme Court.

C. A court may order that the privilege or protection is not waived by the disclosure connected with the litigation pending before the court, in which case the disclosure does not operate as a waiver in any other proceeding.

D. An agreement on the effect of the disclosure in a proceeding is binding only on the parties to the agreement, unless it is incorporated into a court order.

E. This section shall not limit any otherwise applicable waiver of attorney-client privilege or work product protection by an inmate who files an action challenging his conviction or sentence.

VA. R. EV. 2:502. ATTORNEY-CLIENT PRIVILEGE

Except as may be provided by statute, the existence and application of the attorney-client privilege in Virginia, and the exceptions thereto, shall be governed by the principles of common law as interpreted by the courts of the Commonwealth in the light of reason and experience.

Comparison and Commentary

The federal rules of evidence contain a lengthy rule added in 2008 that addresses the inadvertent production of material protected by the attorney-client privilege. The Virginia evidence rules do not include such a provision, although the state enacted a statute paralleling the federal rule in 2010. See VA Code § 8.01–420.7 (reprinted above). Rather than incorporate this statute as Rule 2:502, the Virginia codifiers employ Rule 2:502 for a generic statement affirming the common-law status of attorney-client privilege.

Attorney-Client Privilege

Both the Virginia and federal courts recognize a non-statutory attorney-client privilege through judicial decisions. See Owens-Corning Fiberglas Corp. v. Watson, 243 Va. 128, 141, 413 S.E.2d 630, 638 (1992) ("Confidential communications between attorney and client made during the course of the relationship and that relate to the subject matter of the attorney's employment are privileged from disclosure. … This privilege exists between a corporation and its in-house attorney.") (citing Upjohn Co. v. U.S., 449 U.S. 383, 389-90 (1981)). Given the breadth of attorney-client privilege doctrine, distinctions between federal and Virginia court rulings are inevitable, but the basic thrust of the privilege is the same in both systems, as cites within Virginia case law to federal decisions indicate. The similarities also extend to "work-product doctrine." The Virginia Supreme Court has explained:

> The work product doctrine is closely related to the attorney-client privilege. Generally, material such as "interviews, statements, memoranda, correspondence, briefs, mental impressions, [and] personal beliefs," which are "prepared by an adversary's counsel with an eye toward litigation" may be free from discovery. Hickman v. Taylor, 329 U.S. 495, 511, 67 S.Ct. 385, 393–394, 91 L.Ed. 451 (1947).

Com. v. Edwards, 235 Va. 499, 510, 370 S.E.2d 296, 302 (1988).

Inadvertent Disclosure

As in the federal system, the Virginia Supreme Court has held that attorney-client privilege waiver through inadvertent production "may occur if the disclosing party failed to take reasonable measures to ensure and maintain the document's confidentiality, or to take prompt and reasonable steps to rectify the error." Walton v. Mid-Atl. Spine Specialists, 280 Va. 113, 126-27, 694 S.E.2d 545, 552 (2010). The Court advises that a trial court deciding whether a waiver has occurred should consider five factors:

> "(1) the reasonableness of the precautions to prevent inadvertent disclosures, (2) the time taken to rectify the error, (3) the scope of the discovery, (4) the extent of the disclosure, and (5) whether the party asserting the claim of privilege or protection for the communication has used its unavailability for misleading or

otherwise improper or overreaching purposes in the litigation, making it unfair to allow the party to invoke confidentiality under the circumstances." Id.

Shortly after *Walton*, the Virginia General Assembly enacted the statutory provision reprinted above that codifies the *Walton* framework.

VA. R. EV. 2:503. CLERGY AND COMMUNICANT PRIVILEGE (derived from Code §§ 8.01-400 and 19.2-271.3)

A clergy member means any regular minister, priest, rabbi, or accredited practitioner over the age of 18 years, of any religious organization or denomination usually referred to as a church. A clergy member shall not be required:

(a) in any civil action, to give testimony as a witness or to disclose in discovery proceedings the contents of notes, records or any written documentation made by the clergy member, where such testimony or disclosure would reveal any information communicated in a confidential manner, properly entrusted to such clergy member in a professional capacity and necessary to enable discharge of the functions of office according to the usual course of the clergy member's practice or discipline, wherein the person so communicating such information about himself or herself, or another, was seeking spiritual counsel and advice relating to and growing out of the information so imparted; and

(b) in any criminal action, in giving testimony as a witness to disclose any information communicated by the accused in a confidential manner, properly entrusted to the clergy member in a professional capacity and necessary to enable discharge of the functions of office according to the usual course of the clergy member's practice or discipline, where the person so communicating such information about himself or herself, or another, was seeking spiritual counsel and advice relating to and growing out of the information so imparted.

Comparison and Commentary

The federal courts recognize a privilege that protects disclosure of "communications made (1) to a clergyperson (2) in his or her spiritual and professional capacity (3) with a reasonable expectation of confidentiality." In re Grand Jury Investigation, 918 F.2d 374, 384 (3d Cir. 1990) (recognizing and sketching contours of privilege). Virginia also recognizes this privilege in Rule 2:503. Although federal case law is sparse, a significant distinction between Virginia and federal privilege law in this context concerns the holder of the privilege. In the federal system, the lay person (penitent) holds the privilege. Virginia law, by contrast, "plainly invests the priest with the privilege and leaves it to his conscience to decide when disclosure is appropriate." Seidman v. Fishburne-Hudgins Educ. Found., 724 F.2d 413, 416 (4th Cir. 1984). Virginia's privilege is also significantly narrowed in criminal cases, where the privilege only applies if the communication was made by the accused. Rule 2:503(b).

VA. R. EV. 2:504. SPOUSAL TESTIMONY AND MARITAL COMMUNICATIONS PRIVILEGES (Rule 2:504(a) derived from Code § 8.01-398; and Rule 2:504(b) derived from Code § 19.2-271.2)

(a) Privileged Marital Communications in Civil Cases.

1. Husband and wife shall be competent witnesses to testify for or against each other in all civil actions.

2. In any civil proceeding, a person has a privilege to refuse to disclose, and to prevent anyone else from disclosing, any confidential communication between such person and his or her spouse during their marriage, regardless of whether such person is married to that spouse at the time he or she

objects to disclosure. This privilege may not be asserted in any proceeding in which the spouses are adverse parties, or in which either spouse is charged with a crime or tort against the person or property of the other or against the minor child of either spouse. For the purposes of this Rule, "confidential communication" means a communication made privately by a person to his or her spouse that is not intended for disclosure to any other person.

(b) Testimony of Husband and Wife in Criminal Cases.

1. In criminal cases husband and wife shall be allowed, and, subject to the Rules of Evidence governing other witnesses, may be compelled to testify in behalf of each other, but neither shall be compelled to be called as a witness against the other, except (i) in the case of a prosecution for an offense committed by one against the other, against a minor child of either, or against the property of either; (ii) in any case where either is charged with forgery of the name of the other or uttering or attempting to utter a writing bearing the allegedly forged signature of the other; or (iii) in any proceeding relating to a violation of the laws pertaining to criminal sexual assault (§§ 18.2-61 through 18.2-67.10), crimes against nature (§ 18.2-361) involving a minor as a victim and provided the defendant and the victim are not married to each other, incest (§ 18.2-366), or abuse of children (§§ 18.2-370 through 18.2-371). The failure of either husband or wife to testify, however, shall create no presumption against the accused, nor be the subject of any comment before the court or jury by any attorney.

2. Except in the prosecution for a criminal offense as set forth in subsections (B)(1)(i), (ii) and (iii) above, in any criminal proceeding, a person has a privilege to refuse to disclose, and to prevent anyone else from disclosing, any

confidential communication between such person and his or her spouse during their marriage, regardless of whether the person is married to that spouse at the time the person objects to disclosure. For the purposes of this Rule, "confidential communication" means a communication made privately by a person to his or her spouse that is not intended for disclosure to any other person.

Comparison and Commentary

The federal rules of evidence do not contain any marital privilege. The federal courts have, however, recognized a marital privilege under the authority of Rule 501. Like Virginia, the federal courts recognize both a spousal testimonial privilege and a spousal communication privilege.

Spousal Testimonial Privilege

The United States Supreme Court has established a federal privilege that enables a person to refuse to testify adversely against his or her spouse, a privilege generally referred to as the "spousal testimonial privilege." Trammel v. U.S., 445 U.S. 40, 53 (1980) ("the witness-spouse alone has a privilege to refuse to testify adversely; the witness may be neither compelled to testify nor foreclosed from testifying"). Virginia recognizes a similar privilege in Rule 2:504(b)(1). Virginia's testimonial privilege applies by its terms only in criminal cases. The federal privilege is generally invoked in criminal cases; its application in civil cases remains an open question. See In re Martenson, 779 F.2d 461, 463 (8th Cir. 1985) (recognizing, but not addressing question). Both privileges apply only to "adverse" testimony. *Trammel* at 51; Rule 2:504(b)(1). Both the federal and Virginia privilege contain exceptions, most notably where the spouse is the victim of a charged crime or the victim is a child of either spouse. *Trammel* at 46 n.7 (noting exceptions "for cases in which one spouse commits a crime against the other"; "crimes against the spouse's property"; and "crimes against children of either spouse"). Virginia's rule includes even broader exceptions, such as a provision that the privilege does not apply in prosecutions for "a violation of the laws pertaining to criminal sexual assault." See Rule 2:504(b)(1)(ii)-(iii).

Spousal Communication Privilege

The United States Supreme Court has also established a federal privilege that allows a person to prevent the introduction into evidence of a confidential communication between that person and a spouse made during their marriage, i.e., a "spousal communication privilege." See *Trammel* at 45 n.5 (citing Wolfle v. U.S., 291 U.S. 7 (1934)). Virginia's spousal communication privilege is found in Rules 2:504(a)(2) and (b)(2). The spousal communication privilege applies in civil and criminal cases. Both the Virginia and federal spousal communication privilege include the exceptions discussed in the context of the spousal testimonial privilege. See *Trammel* at 46 n.7 (recognizing "[s]imilar exceptions"); Rule 2:504(a)(2) and (b)(2). As with the spousal testimonial privilege, Virginia's spousal communication privilege contains additional carve outs for certain criminal cases. Rule 2:504(b)(2).

There is Virginia case law suggesting that the spousal communication privilege applies beyond "communications," to "information" known by the spouse more generally, see Menefee v. Com., 189 Va. 900, 912, 55 S.E.2d 9, 15 (1949), but the Virginia Supreme Court has more recently suggested that the narrower statutory language controls. Burns v. Com., 261 Va. 307, 333, 541 S.E.2d 872, 890 (2001) ("[T]he plain words utilized in this statutory provision limit the privilege to situations where a spouse ... is revealing a private communication through testimony."); Rule 2:504(a)(2) and (b)(2) ("confidential communication").

VA. R. EV. 2:505. HEALING ARTS PRACTITIONER AND PATIENT PRIVILEGE (derived from Code § 8.01-399)

The scope and application of the privilege between a patient and a physician or practitioner of the healing arts in a civil case shall be as set forth in any specific statutory provisions, including Code § 8.01-399, as amended from time to time, which presently provides:

A. Except at the request or with the consent of the patient, or as provided in this section, no duly licensed practitioner of any branch of the healing arts shall be permitted to testify in any civil action, respecting any information that he may have acquired in attending, examining or treating the patient in a professional capacity.

B. If the physical or mental condition of the patient is at issue in a civil action, the diagnoses, signs and symptoms, observations, evaluations, histories, or treatment plan of the practitioner, obtained or formulated as contemporaneously documented during the course of the practitioner's treatment, together with the facts communicated to, or otherwise learned by, such practitioner in connection with such attendance, examination or treatment shall be disclosed but only in discovery pursuant to the Rules of Court or through testimony at the trial of the action. In addition, disclosure may be ordered when a court, in the exercise of sound discretion, deems it necessary to the proper administration of justice. However, no order shall be entered compelling a party to sign a release for medical records from a health care provider unless the health care provider is not located in the Commonwealth or is a federal facility. If an order is issued pursuant to this section, it shall be restricted to the medical records that relate to the physical or mental conditions at issue in the case. No disclosure of diagnosis or treatment plan facts communicated to, or otherwise learned by, such practitioner shall occur if the court determines, upon the request of the patient, that such facts are not relevant to the subject matter involved in the pending action or do not appear to be reasonably calculated to lead to the discovery of admissible evidence. Only diagnosis offered to a reasonable degree of medical probability shall be admissible at trial.

C. This section shall not (i) be construed to repeal or otherwise affect the provisions of § 65.2-607 relating to privileged communications between physicians and surgeons and employees under the Workers' Compensation Act; (ii) apply to information communicated to any such practitioner in an effort unlawfully to procure a narcotic drug, or unlawfully to procure the administration of any such drug; or (iii) prohibit a duly licensed practitioner of the healing arts, or his agents, from disclosing information as required by state or federal law.

D. Neither a lawyer nor anyone acting on the lawyer's behalf shall obtain, in connection with pending or threatened litigation, information concerning a patient from a practitioner of any branch of the healing arts without the consent of the patient, except through discovery pursuant to the Rules of Supreme Court as herein provided. However, the prohibition of this subsection shall not apply to:

1. Communication between a lawyer retained to represent a practitioner of the healing arts, or that lawyer's agent, and that practitioner's employers, partners, agents, servants, employees, co-employees or others for whom, at law, the practitioner is or may be liable or who, at law, are or may be liable for the practitioner's acts or omissions;

2. Information about a patient provided to a lawyer or his agent by a practitioner of the healing arts employed by that lawyer to examine or evaluate the patient in accordance with Rule 4:10 of the Rules of Supreme Court;

or

3. Contact between a lawyer or his agent and a nonphysician employee or agent of a practitioner of healing arts for any of the following purposes: (i) scheduling appearances, (ii) requesting a written recitation by the practitioner of handwritten records obtained by the lawyer or his agent from the practitioner, provided the request is made in writing and, if litigation is pending, a copy of the request and the practitioner's response is provided simultaneously to the patient or his attorney, (iii) obtaining information necessary to obtain service upon the practitioner in pending litigation, (iv) determining when records summoned will be provided by the practitioner or his agent, (v) determining what patient records the practitioner possesses in order to summons records in pending litigation, (vi) explaining any summons that the lawyer or his agent caused to be issued and served on the practitioner, (vii) verifying dates the practitioner treated the patient, provided that if litigation is pending the information obtained by the lawyer or his agent is promptly given, in writing, to the patient or his attorney, (viii) determining charges by the practitioner for appearance at a deposition or to testify before any tribunal or administrative body, or (ix) providing to or obtaining from the practitioner directions to a place to which he is or will be summoned to give testimony.

E. A clinical psychologist duly licensed under the provisions of Chapter 36 (§ 54.1-3600 et seq.) of Title 54.1 shall be considered a practitioner of a branch of the healing arts within the meaning of this section.

F. Nothing herein shall prevent a duly licensed practitioner of the healing arts, or his agents, from disclosing any information that he may have acquired in attending, examining or treating a patient in a professional capacity where such disclosure is necessary in connection with the care of the patient, the protection or enforcement of a practitioner's legal rights including such rights with respect to medical malpractice actions, or the operations of a health care facility or health maintenance organization or in order to comply with state or federal law.

Comparison and Commentary

Like many states, Virginia affords a privilege to a patient to block disclosure of statements made by the patient to a "practitioner of the healing arts." The privilege applies only in civil cases. Rule 2:505(A). There is no such privilege in the federal system. See, e.g., Hancock v. Dodson, 958 F.2d 1367, 1373 (6th Cir. 1992) ("[T]he federal courts do not recognize a federal physician-patient privilege.") For a discussion of the federal psychotherapist-patient privilege, see Comparison and Commentary to Rule 2:506.

VA. R. EV. 2:506. MENTAL HEALTH PROFESSIONAL AND CLIENT PRIVILEGE (derived from Code § 8.01-400.2)

Except at the request of or with the consent of the client, no licensed professional counselor, as defined in Code §54.1-3500; licensed clinical social worker, as defined in Code §54.1-3700; licensed psychologist, as defined in Code §54.1-3600; or licensed marriage and family therapist, as defined in Code §54.1-3500, shall be required in giving testimony as a witness in any civil action to disclose any information communicated in a confidential manner, properly entrusted to such person in a professional capacity and necessary to enable discharge of professional or occupational services according to the usual course of his or her practice or discipline, wherein the person so communicating such information about himself or herself, or another, is seeking professional counseling or treatment and advice relating to and growing out of the information so imparted; provided, however, that when the physical or mental condition of the client is at issue in such action, or when a court, in the exercise of sound discretion, deems such disclosure necessary to the proper administration of justice, no fact communicated to, or otherwise learned by, such practitioner in connection with such counseling, treatment or advice shall be privileged, and disclosure may be required. The privileges conferred by this Rule shall not extend to testimony in matters relating to child abuse and neglect nor serve to relieve any person from the reporting requirements set forth in §63.2-1509.

Comparison and Commentary

Both the Virginia rules and the United States Supreme Court recognize a psychotherapist-patient privilege. Jaffee v. Redmond, 518 U.S. 1, 15 (1996) ("[C]onfidential communications between a licensed psychotherapist and her patients in the course of diagnosis or treatment are protected from compelled disclosure.") Both the federal and Virginia privileges apply broadly to the various types of mental health counselors, not solely psychiatrists and psychologists. See *Jaffee* at 15; Rule 2:506. Both the federal and Virginia privilege give way to varying degrees when the patient's mental state is "in issue." Rule 2:506. As the federal decisions are not uniform on this point, generalization is unhelpful.

The Virginia privilege found in Rule 2:506 and Rule 2:505(E) is much narrower than the federal variant. First, the Virginia privilege applies only in civil cases. Second, the Virginia privilege gives way "when a court, in the exercise of sound discretion, deems such disclosure necessary to the proper administration of justice," an escape valve explicitly rejected by the federal Supreme Court. Jaffee, 518 U.S. at 17 & n. 18 ("reject[ing] the balancing component of the privilege implemented by ... a small number of States," including Virginia). The Virginia privilege also does not apply in "matters relating to child abuse and neglect."

VA. R. EV. 2:507. PRIVILEGED COMMUNICATIONS INVOLVING INTERPRETERS (derived from Code §§ 8.01-400.1, 19.2-164, and 19.2-164.1)

Whenever a deaf or non-English-speaking person communicates through an interpreter to any person under such circumstances that the communication would be privileged, and such person could not be compelled to testify as to the communications, the privilege shall also apply to the interpreter.

Comparison and Commentary

Virginia Rule 2:507 states that a communication that would be privileged but for the presence of a necessary interpreter is also privileged. A similar principle can be found in the federal system. See United States v. Massachusetts Inst. of Tech., 129 F.3d 681, 684 (1st Cir. 1997) ("[D]ecisions do tend to mark out, although not with perfect consistency, a small circle of 'others' with whom information may be shared without loss of the privilege (e.g., secretaries, interpreters, counsel for a cooperating co-defendant, a parent present when a child consults a lawyer)").

ARTICLE VI. WITNESSES

FED. R. EV. 601. COMPETENCY TO TESTIFY IN GENERAL

Every person is competent to be a witness unless these rules provide otherwise. But in a civil case, state law governs the witness's competency regarding a claim or defense for which state law supplies the rule of decision.

VA. R. EV. 2:601. GENERAL RULE OF COMPETENCY

(a) Generally. Every person is competent to be a witness except as otherwise provided in other evidentiary principles, Rules of Court, Virginia statutes, or common law.

(b) Rulings. A court may declare a person incompetent to testify if the court finds that the person does not have sufficient physical or mental capacity to testify truthfully, accurately, or understandably.

Comparison and Commentary

Both the federal and Virginia rules contain provisions addressing witness competency. The federal rule, described by the Advisory Committee as a "general ground-clearing," eliminates the once-prominent common-law competency rules. The Virginia Rule does much the same in Rule 2:601(a). Virginia adds subsection (b), however, providing explicit authority for judges to declare witnesses incompetent. The resulting distinction is one of degree rather than kind.

The federal rule signals disfavor of court findings that witnesses are incompetent, creating, in effect, a strong presumption of competency. See also 18 U.S.C. § 3509(c)(4) ("A competency examination regarding a child may be conducted only if the court determines, on the record, that compelling reasons exist. A child's age alone is not a compelling reason.") Still, that does not mean that federal judges are unable to bar witnesses on the grounds of competency. See U.S. v. Lightly, 677 F.2d 1027, 1028 (4th Cir. 1982) ("Every witness is presumed competent to testify, Fed.R.Evid. 601, unless it can be shown that the witness does not have personal knowledge of the matters about which he is to testify, that he does not have the capacity to recall, or that he does not understand the duty to testify truthfully.")

The Virginia rule contemplates a more active role for trial judges in assessing witness competency, but the ultimate standards are essentially the same. Ortiz v. Com., 276 Va. 705, 720, 667 S.E.2d 751, 760 (Va. 2008) (explaining that "[i]t is the trial judge's duty to determine the competency of a child witness after 'a careful examination of the child'" but rejecting challenge to finding of competency); Turnbull v. Com., 216 Va. 328, 334, 218 S.E.2d 541, 546 (Va. 1975) ("It is the function of the trial court to determine whether a witness is competent, that is, whether the witness possesses such understanding as to remember events and a knowledge of right and wrong."); see also VA Code § 8.01-396 (declaring that parties and interested persons are not incompetent and can testify and that courts may require such persons to testify in court); VA Code § 8.01-396.1 ("No child shall be deemed incompetent to testify solely because of age.").

FED. R. EV. 602. NEED FOR PERSONAL KNOWLEDGE

A witness may testify to a matter only if evidence is introduced sufficient to support a finding that the witness has personal knowledge of the matter. Evidence to prove personal knowledge may consist of the witness's own testimony. This rule does not apply to a witness's expert testimony under Rule 703.

VA. R. EV. 2:602. LACK OF PERSONAL KNOWLEDGE

A witness may not testify to a matter unless evidence is introduced sufficient to support a finding that the witness has personal knowledge of the matter. Evidence to prove personal knowledge may, but need not, consist of the testimony of the witness. This Rule does not bar testimony admissible under Rules 2:701, 2-702 and 2:703.

Comparison and Commentary

The Virginia and federal rules requiring witnesses, other than experts, to testify based on personal knowledge are virtually identical. The Virginia rule references the rules governing lay and expert opinion testimony as exceptions to the principle, while the federal rule only references the rule governing expert opinion testimony. No substantive difference follows from this distinction, since the lay opinion rule (Rule 701) is the same in both systems.

FED. R. EV. 603. OATH OR AFFIRMATION TO TESTIFY TRUTHFULLY

Before testifying, a witness must give an oath or affirmation to testify truthfully. It must be in a form designed to impress that duty on the witness's conscience.

VA. R. EV. 2:603. OATH OR AFFIRMATION

Before testifying, every witness shall be required to declare that he or she will testify truthfully, by oath or affirmation administered in a form calculated to awaken the conscience and impress the mind of the witness with the duty to do so.

Comparison and Commentary

Both the Virginia and federal rules require witnesses to testify under oath or affirmation.

FED. R. EV. 604. INTERPRETER

An interpreter must be qualified and must give an oath or affirmation to make a true translation.

VA. R. EV. 2:604. INTERPRETERS (derived from Code § 8.01-406)

An interpreter shall be qualified as competent and shall be placed under oath or affirmation to make a true translation.

Comparison and Commentary

Both the Virginia and federal rules contain a provision authorizing competent, sworn interpreters. Va. Code § 19.2-164 provides for necessary translation in criminal trials. See also Va. Code § 8.01-406 (requiring that interpreters "be sworn" and allowing judge to require "testimony of a deaf individual and the interpretation thereof to be visually electronically recorded").

FED. R. EV. 605. JUDGE'S COMPETENCY AS A WITNESS

The presiding judge may not testify as a witness at the trial. A party need not object to preserve the issue.

VA. R. EV. 2:605. COMPETENCY OF COURT PERSONNEL AS WITNESSES (derived from Code § 19.2-271)

(a) No judge shall be competent to testify in any criminal or civil proceeding as to any matter which came before the judge in the course of official duties.

(b) No clerk of any court, magistrate, or other person having the power to issue warrants, shall be competent to testify in any criminal or civil proceeding, except proceedings wherein the defendant is charged with perjury, as to any matter which came before him or her in the course of official duties. Such person shall be competent to testify in any criminal proceeding wherein the defendant is charged pursuant to the provisions of §18.2-460 [ed. – obstructing court officer] or in any proceeding authorized pursuant to §19.2-353.3 [ed. – failure to pay court fines]. Notwithstanding any other provision of this section, any judge, clerk of any court, magistrate, or other person having the power to issue warrants, who is the victim of a crime, shall not be incompetent solely because of his or her office to testify in any criminal or civil proceeding arising out of the crime. Nothing in this subpart (b) shall preclude otherwise proper testimony by a clerk or deputy clerk concerning documents filed in the official records.

Comparison and Commentary

Federal Rule 605 prohibits judges from testifying in trials over which they preside and relieves the parties of any obligation of objecting should a judge attempt to do so. Virginia Rule 2:605 is much broader in two respects. First, it prevents judges from testifying in any proceeding (not just in the trial over which the judge is presiding) about matters that came before them in their judicial role. Second, it extends to other judicial employees such as clerks – and perhaps beyond. Tidewater Constr. Corp. v. Pretlow, 0806-96-1, 1996 WL 653394 (Va. App. 1996) (unpublished) (holding that a "deputy commissioner employed by the [workers' compensation] commission is an 'other person,' prohibited ... from testifying" under this rule).

The evil contemplated by the Virginia statute is unclear. Perhaps the statute is intended to ensure that judges incorporate all explanations of their decisions into those actions themselves. See Bartlett v. Bank of Carroll, 218 Va. 240, 248, 237 S.E.2d 115, 120 (Va. 1977) ("Judge Matthews should not have been allowed to testify and to explain or to interpret the meaning of the November 23, 1973 decree which he entered.") But Virginia's rule has the potential to create lots of mischief. One potential problem is alleviated by the exception allowing clerks to testify regarding official records. Still, many minefields remain. Clearly, the statute should not be read to disqualify judges from testifying about matters related, but nonetheless, tangential to their official duties. Bennett v. Com., 3047-05-2, 2007 WL 1119801 (Va. App. 2007) (unpublished) ("[A] judge who passively witnesses conduct [even while on the job] not coming before him for adjudication is not incompetent to testify under the statute where he is 'a disinterested witness who merely happened to observe' the conduct at issue.") There are, however, times when a judge participates in a matter and would logically be expected to testify about it. A primary example arises in challenges to contempt proceedings, as was at issue in Epps v. Com., 47 Va. App. 687, 701, 626 S.E.2d 912, 918 (Va. App. 2006). In *Epps*, the Court of Appeals ruled that a judge could not testify in a contempt proceeding that followed a dispute between the judge and the sheriff regarding court security. The Virginia Supreme Court affirmed the only portion of the ruling that was challenged in Com. v. Epps, 273 Va. 410, 414, 641 S.E.2d 77, 80 (Va. 2007), holding that the exception in Rule 2:605(b) for judges who are crime victims did not apply.

A similar problem arises if a district judge finds someone in contempt summarily, and the person appeals the finding to a circuit court, as is permitted in the Virginia system, for trial de novo. It would appear from section 19.2–271, that the district judge would be prohibited from testifying to support the contempt finding. An awkward resolution to this dilemma comes through a certificate provision that accompanies the circuit court appeal right. VA Code § 18.2-459 ("Any person sentenced to pay a fine, or to confinement, [via summary contempt in the district court], may appeal therefrom to the circuit court.... If such appeal be taken, a certificate of the conviction and the particular circumstances of the offense, together with the recognizance, shall forthwith be transmitted by the sentencing judge to the clerk of such circuit court, who shall immediately deliver the same to the judge thereof. Such judge, sitting without a jury, shall hear the case upon the certificate and any legal testimony adduced on either side, and make such order therein as may seem to him proper."); Baugh v. Com., 14 Va. App. 368, 372, 417 S.E.2d 891, 894 (Va. App. 1992) ("Oftentimes, however, the district court judge is an indispensable witness to the contemptuous event and his or her testimony is essential to prosecution of the offense on an appeal. Code § 18.2–459 resolves this dilemma by requiring that the district court judge submit a 'certificate of the conviction and the particular circumstances of the offense.'"). The Supreme Court indicated generic disapproval of *Baugh*, but appears to agree with the case on the point discussed above. Gilman v. Com., 275 Va. 222, 230-31, 657 S.E.2d 474, 478 (Va. 2008) ("Under Code § 18.2–459, however, a circuit court judge hearing an appeal of a summary contempt adjudication may consider as evidence the district court judge's factual summary of the events that occurred during the district court proceedings.")

FED. R. EV. 606. JUROR'S COMPETENCY AS A WITNESS

(a) At the Trial. A juror may not testify as a witness before the other jurors at the trial. If a juror is called to testify, the court must give a party an opportunity to object outside the jury's presence.

(b) During an Inquiry Into the Validity of a Verdict or Indictment.

(1) Prohibited Testimony or Other Evidence. During an inquiry into the validity of a verdict or indictment, a juror may not testify about any statement made or incident that occurred during the jury's deliberations; the effect of anything on that juror's or another juror's vote; or any

juror's mental processes concerning the verdict or
indictment. The court may not receive a juror's affidavit or
evidence of a juror's statement on these matters.

(2) Exceptions. A juror may testify about whether:

(A) extraneous prejudicial information was
improperly brought to the jury's attention;

(B) an outside influence was improperly brought to
bear on any juror; or

(C) a mistake was made in entering the verdict on
the verdict form.

VA. R. EV. 2:606. COMPETENCY OF JUROR AS WITNESS

Upon inquiry regarding the validity of a verdict or indictment,
a juror is precluded from testifying as to any matter or
statement occurring during the course of the jury's
deliberations or to the effect of anything upon any juror's mind
or emotions as influencing any juror to assent to or dissent
from the verdict or indictment or concerning any juror's mental
processes in connection therewith.

A juror may testify only as to questions regarding extraneous
prejudicial information improperly brought to the jury's
attention as a result of conduct outside the jury room, or
whether any improper influence was brought to bear upon any
juror from a source outside the jury room.

Comparison and Commentary

Both the Virginia and federal rules prohibit anyone from introducing
evidence from a juror about jury deliberations for purposes of
challenging the validity of a verdict or grand jury indictment. Tanner

v. U.S., 483 U.S. 107, 118 (1987) (discussing federal prohibition); Caterpillar Tractor Co. v. Hulvey, 233 Va. 77, 82, 353 S.E.2d 747, 750-51 (Va. 1987) (explaining general rule that "the testimony of jurors should not be received to impeach their verdict, especially on the ground of their own misconduct" and that exceptions to the rule are generally limited to "activities of jurors that occur outside the jury room," particularly where "misconduct outside the jury room has prejudicially affected the jury's deliberation of the case by injecting facts connected with the case which had not been admitted in evidence"); Evans-Smith v. Com., 5 Va. App. 188, 209, 361 S.E.2d 436, 448 (Va. App. 1987) (concluding that bar to juror testimony did not apply because "the alleged misconduct was not the jurors' mental processes, but ... evidence, aliunde, which may have influenced their mental processes").

The federal rule includes a sentence that extends the prohibition on juror testimony to any evidence that relates juror statements (e.g., affidavits or press reports). The Virginia rule only prohibits juror "testi[mony]." This distinction has not been tested in Virginia's courts, although case law supports the proposition that affidavits can be offered to prompt an investigation. Com. Union Ins. v. Moorefield, 231 Va. 260, 265, 343 S.E.2d 329, 333 (Va. 1986) (noting that "an affidavit [about juror misconduct] may be sufficient to require the trial court to investigate the matters recited in the document"). Of course, the inability to introduce juror testimony will eventually lead to proof problems, primarily based on the hearsay bar. Id.; Evans-Smith v. Com., 5 Va. App. 188, 207, 361 S.E.2d 436, 447 (Va. App. 1987) ("A motion for a new trial based on juror misconduct cannot be sustained on juror affidavits alone.") In addition, if affidavits (or other evidence) merely relate misconduct internal to the deliberations, no investigation is warranted. Jenkins v. Com., 244 Va. 445, 460, 423 S.E.2d 360, 370 (Va. 1992) (rejecting challenge based on press reports of jury misconduct because "any alleged misconduct, if it occurred, was clearly within the confines of the jury room" and consequently, "a post-trial investigation into the allegations was unwarranted"). In practice, the federal prohibition is likely no different from Virginia in this regard. Although technically affidavits falling under the prohibition cannot be "received" by a federal court under Rule 606, the court will still need to review the affidavit to determine its admissibility. See Tanner v. U.S., 483 U.S. 107, 125 (1987) (drawing conclusions about legal challenge based on "affidavits and testimony presented in support of the first new trial motion").

The federal rule contains two other provisions that are not included in the Virginia rule: (1) the federal rule provides an exception for testimony about a mistake in entering the verdict on the verdict form, 606(b)(2)(C); (2) the federal rule contains a provision, 606(a), prohibiting jurors from testifying in front of the other jurors in the trial.

The first distinction arises from a 2006 amendment to the original federal rule, which added Rule 606(b)(2)(C) to respond to "a divergence between the text of the rule and case law that has established an exception for proof of clerical errors." Advisory Committee Note to 2006 Amendment. Virginia case law does not address the question of whether jurors could testify about an error in entering the verdict on the verdict form. A literal application of Rule 2:206 would prohibit such testimony. One imagines that a court confronted with a compelling case that a guilty verdict had been entered in error by the jury would find some means of correcting the injustice. Cf. Bazemore v. Com., 42 Va. App. 203, 212, 590 S.E.2d 602, 606 (Va. App. 2004) (remanding criminal case to "trial court for the limited purpose of correcting [a trial court's] error in the verdict form"). Virginia does provide defendants a right to poll the jury upon a guilty verdict so the issue should come up rarely if at all. See Va. Sup. Ct. Rule 3A:17(d); Humbert v. Com., 29 Va. App. 783, 792, 514 S.E.2d 804, 808 (Va. App. 1999) ("a defendant has a right to have the jury 'polled individually,' to confirm that each juror joins in the verdict and that it is, in fact, unanimous" and discussing trial court's responsibilities when jurors express confusion).

The second distinction – juror testimony – is also without discussion in Virginia case law. This should not be surprising as it would certainly be an unusual event for a juror to be called to testify in front of his or her fellow jurors.

FED. R. EV. 607. WHO MAY IMPEACH A WITNESS

Any party, including the party that called the witness, may attack the witness's credibility.

VA. R. EV. 2:607. IMPEACHMENT OF WITNESSES
(Rule 2:607(b) derived from Code § 8.01-401(A); and Rule 2:607(c) derived from Code § 8.01-403)

(a) In general. Subject to the provisions of Rule 2:403, the credibility of a witness may be impeached by any party other than the one calling the witness, with any proof that is relevant to the witness's credibility. Impeachment may be undertaken, among other means, by:

> (i) introduction of evidence of the witness's bad general reputation for the traits of truth and veracity, as provided in Rule 2:608(a) and (b);

> (ii) evidence of prior conviction, as provided in Rule 2:609;

> (iii) evidence of prior unadjudicated perjury, as provided in Rule 2:608(d);

> (iv) evidence of prior false accusations of sexual misconduct, as provided in Rule 2:608(e);

> (v) evidence of bias as provided in Rule 2:610;

> (vi) prior inconsistent statements as provided in 2:613;

> (vii) contradiction by other evidence; and

(viii) any other evidence which is probative on the issue of credibility because of a logical tendency to convince the trier of fact that the witness's perception, memory, or narration is defective or impaired, or that the sincerity or veracity of the witness is questionable.

Impeachment pursuant to subdivisions (a)(i) and (ii) of this Rule may not be undertaken by a party who has called an adverse witness.

(b) Witness with adverse interest. A witness having an adverse interest may be examined with leading questions by the party calling the witness. After such an adverse direct examination, the witness is subject to cross-examination.

(c) Witness proving adverse.

(i) If a witness proves adverse, the party who called the witness may, subject to the discretion of the court, prove that the witness has made at other times a statement inconsistent with the present testimony as provided in Rule 2:613.

(ii) In a jury case, if impeachment has been conducted pursuant to this subdivision (c), the court, on motion by either party, shall instruct the jury to consider the evidence of such inconsistent statements solely for the purpose of contradicting the witness.

Comparison and Commentary

The federal rules permit parties to freely impeach their own witnesses, allowing those who encounter this rule to rejoice at its simplicity and move on to other matters. Virginia litigants are not so lucky.

With respect to "any party other than the one calling the witness,"

Rule 2:607(a) provides a non-exclusive list of methods of permissible impeachment, cross-referencing other areas of the rules where pertinent. These methods of impeachment are familiar and, as indicated by the cross-references, would be permissible regardless of their endorsement here.

Virginia's rules are different for the party who calls the witness. The limits on impeachment in this circumstance derive, in part, from two dusty statutes. See Va. Code § 8.01-403 ("A party producing a witness shall not be allowed to impeach his credit by general evidence of bad character, but he may, in case the witness shall in the opinion of the court prove adverse, by leave of the court, prove that he has made at other times a statement inconsistent with his present testimony."); Va. Code § 8.01-401(A) ("A party called to testify for another, having an adverse interest, may be examined by such other party according to the rules applicable to cross-examination.") It is clear from the first statute that a party calling a witness cannot attack the witness' character for truthfulness. Smith v. Lohr, 204 Va. 331, 335, 130 S.E.2d 433, 436 (1963). This explains the last proviso in Rule 2:607(a), prohibiting impeachment of one's own "adverse witness" by prior conviction or bad reputation. Logic would extend this prohibition to impeachment under 2:607(a)(iii) and (a)(iv), as they are also character-based credibility attacks.

From here, things get complicated (in large part because the case law, and thus the rule drawn from it, is unclear). Rule 2:607(a) and § 801-403 imply (by negative implication) that a party who calls an "adverse witness" can employ non-character based forms of impeachment. Rule 2:607(b) echoes § 8.01-401(A) in stating that a "witness having an adverse interest" may be examined with leading questions. As explained in Maxey v. Com., 26 Va. App. 514, 520-21, 495 S.E.2d 536, 539-40 (1998), "a witness 'having an adverse interest,' ... commonly referred to as an 'adverse witness'" is "an opposing party or a nonparty witness who has a financial or other personal interest in the outcome of the case," such as "persons who are 'closely connected by blood or otherwise to at least one party.'" Importantly, "[a] witness does not have an 'adverse interest' simply because his or her testimony is adverse or injurious to the calling party's case." Id. Left unclear in Rule 2:607's phrasing is whether a party can call a witness who does not satisfy the narrow definition of "adverse witness" quoted above, and then impeach that testimony through non-character impeachment.

Next, Rule 2:607(c)(i), echoing Va. Code § 8.01-403, permits impeachment by prior inconsistent statement when a "witness proves adverse." "The term 'adverse,' under this section, refers to a witness whose testimony is 'injurious or damaging to the case of the party who called the witness.'" Maxey, 26 Va. App. at 519-20, 495 S.E.2d at 539. But, according to Maxey, injurious testimony itself is not enough. "Code § 8.01-403 allows a party to impeach his or her own witness by prior inconsistent statements only when the witness whom the party expected to testify favorably has suddenly given unexpected, adverse testimony on the stand." Id.

Virginia case law contains hints of counsel attempting to sidestep this morass by persuading the judge to call a witness as a "court's witness," a practice still recognized in Rule 2:614, but now only for civil cases. See, e.g., Williams v. Com., 193 Va. 764, 769, 71 S.E.2d 73, 75 (1952) (explaining that "[a]t the suggestion of the attorney for the Commonwealth, and over objection of the accused" a witness was called as a "court's witness," asked a few basic questions by the judge and then "turned over to the Commonwealth's attorney for cross-examination"; and ruling that it was improper to invoke this ploy "simply to permit the Commonwealth to contradict" the witness).

FED. R. EV. 608. A WITNESS'S CHARACTER FOR TRUTHFULNESS OR UNTRUTHFULNESS

(a) Reputation or Opinion Evidence. A witness's credibility may be attacked or supported by testimony about the witness's reputation for having a character for truthfulness or untruthfulness, or by testimony in the form of an opinion about that character. But evidence of truthful character is admissible only after the witness's character for truthfulness has been attacked.

(b) Specific Instances of Conduct. Except for a criminal conviction under Rule 609, extrinsic evidence is not admissible to prove specific instances of a witness's conduct in order to attack or support the witness's character for truthfulness. But the court may, on cross-examination, allow them to be inquired into if they are probative of the character for truthfulness or untruthfulness of:

(1) the witness; or

(2) another witness whose character the witness being cross-examined has testified about.

By testifying on another matter, a witness does not waive any privilege against self-incrimination for testimony that relates only to the witness's character for truthfulness.

VA. R. EV. 2:608. IMPEACHMENT BY EVIDENCE OF REPUTATION FOR TRUTHTELLING AND CONDUCT OF WITNESS

(a) Reputation evidence of the character trait for truthfulness or untruthfulness. The credibility of a witness may be attacked or supported by evidence in the form of reputation, subject to these limitations: (1) the evidence may relate only to character trait for truthfulness or untruthfulness; (2) evidence of truthful character is admissible only after the character trait of the witness for truthfulness has been attacked by reputation evidence or otherwise; and (3) evidence is introduced that the person testifying has sufficient familiarity with the reputation to make the testimony probative.

(b) Specific instances of conduct; extrinsic proof. Except as otherwise provided in this Rule, by other principles of evidence, or by statute, (1) specific instances of the conduct of a witness may not be used to attack or support credibility; and (2) specific instances of the conduct of a witness may not be proved by extrinsic evidence.

(c) Cross-examination of character witness. Specific instances of conduct may, if probative of truthfulness or untruthfulness, be inquired into on cross-examination of a character witness concerning the character trait for truthfulness or untruthfulness of another witness as to whose character trait the witness being cross-examined has testified.

(d) Unadjudicated perjury. If the trial judge makes a threshold determination that a reasonable probability of falsity exists, any witness may be questioned about prior specific instances of unadjudicated perjury. Extrinsic proof of the unadjudicated perjury may not be shown.

(e) Prior false accusations in sexual assault cases. Except as otherwise provided by other evidentiary principles, statutes or Rules of Court, a complaining witness in a sexual assault case may be cross-examined about prior false accusations of sexual misconduct.

Comparison and Commentary

The Virginia and federal rules create an exception to the general ban on propensity evidence for attacks on a witness' character for truthfulness. The federal rule permits testimony in the form of reputation or opinion, while the Virginia rule only allows testimony in the form of reputation. This same distinction between the federal and Virginia Codes repeats in Rule 405 and Rule 2:405.

Both federal and Virginia Rule 608 prohibit the introduction of evidence relating to specific instances of untruthfulness, permitting only cross-examination on such instances. The federal rule allows such cross-examination of both "the witness" – i.e., any person who testifies – as well as "another witness whose character [for truth-telling] the witness being cross-examined has testified about" – i.e., a character witness. The Virginia rule only permits cross-examination on specific instances of the character witness, with two exceptions. First, any witness may be cross-examined about "prior specific instances of unadjudicated perjury." Rule 2:608(d); see Lambert v. Com., 9 Va. App. 67, 71, 383 S.E.2d 752, 754 (Va. App. 1989) ("a witness's credibility may be attacked on cross-examination by inquiry into prior specific instances of unadjudicated acts of perjury"). (Adjudicated perjury resulting in a conviction would be admissible under Rule 2:609.) Second, under Rule 2:608(e), a complaining witness in a sexual assault case can be cross-examined about prior false accusations of sexual misconduct; and extrinsic evidence is permitted to substantiate a charge that a past accusation was false. See Clinebell v. Com., 235 Va. 319, 325, 368 S.E.2d 263, 266 (Va. 1988) ("in a sex crime case, the complaining witness may be cross-examined about prior false accusations, and if the witness denies making the statement, the defense may submit proof of such charges"). As indicated, both exceptions come directly from case law.

The second exception is curious and perhaps worthy of challenge. In jurisdictions where all witnesses can be impeached with prior false statements (as in the federal system), a similar rule that applies to complaining witnesses in sexual assault prosecutions seems defensible. (The courts generally agree that cross-examination or evidence regarding prior *false* allegations of sexual misconduct is not prohibited by Rape Shield laws.) However, in a jurisdiction like Virginia that does not allow any other complaining witness to be cross-examined with a prior false charge, it is less obvious that sexual assault victims should be singled out for this type of cross-examination. The case from which the exception derives, justifies the rule as follows: "In sex offense cases, however, the weight of authority recognizes more liberal rules concerning impeachment of complaining witnesses." *Clinebell* at 265. However, much of the authority cited comes from the Rape Shield context, where the trend is quite the opposite. Modern courts are not, as in *Clinebell*, singling out sexual assault victims for "more liberal" cross-examination, but rather discerning the constitutional boundaries of the degree to which victims can be shielded from it.

Virginia includes a proviso that a witness testifying as to someone's character for truthfulness must have "sufficient familiarity with the reputation to make the testimony probative"; the proviso is absent from the federal rule and likely redundant to Rules 2:401 (relevance), 2:403 (balancing probative value against unfair prejudice, etc.) and 2:602 (personal knowledge).

FED. R. EV. 609. IMPEACHMENT BY EVIDENCE OF A CRIMINAL CONVICTION

(a) In General. The following rules apply to attacking a witness's character for truthfulness by evidence of a criminal conviction:

> (1) for a crime that, in the convicting jurisdiction, was punishable by death or by imprisonment for more than one year, the evidence:

>> (A) must be admitted, subject to Rule 403, in a civil case or in a criminal case in which the witness is not a defendant; and

>> (B) must be admitted in a criminal case in which the witness is a defendant, if the probative value of the evidence outweighs its prejudicial effect to that defendant; and

(2) for any crime regardless of the punishment, the evidence must be admitted if the court can readily determine that establishing the elements of the crime required proving--or the witness's admitting--a dishonest act or false statement.

(b) Limit on Using the Evidence After 10 Years. This subdivision (b) applies if more than 10 years have passed since the witness's conviction or release from confinement for it, whichever is later. Evidence of the conviction is admissible only if:

(1) its probative value, supported by specific facts and circumstances, substantially outweighs its prejudicial effect; and

(2) the proponent gives an adverse party reasonable written notice of the intent to use it so that the party has a fair opportunity to contest its use.

(c) Effect of a Pardon, Annulment, or Certificate of Rehabilitation. Evidence of a conviction is not admissible if:

(1) the conviction has been the subject of a pardon, annulment, certificate of rehabilitation, or other equivalent procedure based on a finding that the person has been rehabilitated, and the person has not been convicted of a later crime punishable by death or by imprisonment for more than one year; or

(2) the conviction has been the subject of a pardon, annulment, or other equivalent procedure based on a finding of innocence.

(d) Juvenile Adjudications. Evidence of a juvenile adjudication is admissible under this rule only if:

(1) it is offered in a criminal case;

(2) the adjudication was of a witness other than the defendant;

(3) an adult's conviction for that offense would be admissible to attack the adult's credibility; and

(4) admitting the evidence is necessary to fairly determine guilt or innocence.

(e) Pendency of an Appeal. A conviction that satisfies this rule is admissible even if an appeal is pending. Evidence of the pendency is also admissible.

VA. R. Ev. 2:609. IMPEACHMENT BY EVIDENCE OF CONVICTION OF CRIME (derived from Code § 19.2-269)

Evidence that a witness has been convicted of a crime may be admitted to impeach the credibility of that witness subject to the following limitations:

(a) Party in a civil case or criminal defendant.

(i) The fact that a party in a civil case or an accused who testifies has previously been convicted of a felony, or a misdemeanor involving moral turpitude, and the number of such convictions may be elicited during examination of the party or accused.

(ii) If a conviction raised under subdivision (a)(i) is denied, it may be proved by extrinsic evidence.

(iii) In any examination pursuant to this subdivision (a), the name or nature of any crime of which the party or accused was convicted, except for perjury, may not be shown, nor may the details of prior convictions be elicited, unless offered to rebut other evidence concerning prior convictions.

(b) Other witnesses. The fact that any other witness has previously been convicted of a felony, or a misdemeanor involving moral turpitude, the number, and the name and nature, but not the details, of such convictions may be elicited during examination of the witness or, if denied, proved by extrinsic evidence.

(c) Juvenile adjudications. Juvenile adjudications may not be used for impeachment of a witness on the subject of general credibility, but may be used to show bias of the witness if constitutionally required.

(d) Adverse Witnesses. A party who calls an adverse witness may not impeach that adverse witness with a prior conviction.

Comparison and Commentary

The federal and Virginia rules allow the credibility of a witness to be impeached with a prior conviction. Significant differences in the rules are discussed below.

Qualifying convictions: The federal rule allows impeachment with any conviction punishable by over a year subject to important and varying, discretionary balancing tests; and admission of all *crimen falsi* convictions (such as embezzlement and perjury) without balancing. Virginia allows impeachment with all felony convictions as well as misdemeanors involving "moral turpitude," without balancing. "Misdemeanor crimes of moral turpitude are limited to those crimes involving lying, cheating and stealing, including making a false statement and petit larceny." Newton v. Com., 29 Va. App. 433, 448, 512 S.E.2d 846, 853 (1999).

Conviction names: Under the federal rule, perceived distinctions in the probative force as impeachment of various convictions warrants introducing the name of the convictions (e.g., "burglary"). See U.S. v. Howell, 285 F.3d 1263, 1267 (10th Cir. 2002). Virginia does not permit names, but instead allows only the fact and "number of [qualifying] convictions" to be introduced if the witness is a party in a civil or criminal case. An exception is made for perjury convictions. The theory in Virginia is that redacting the name of the conviction eases the jury's temptation to use that information beyond its proper purpose. Payne v. Carroll, 250 Va. 336, 339-40, 461 S.E.2d 837, 838 (Va. 1995). In Virginia, redaction takes the place of the balancing test in the federal rules. For non-party witnesses in Virginia, as in the federal system, the name of the conviction can be elicited but not details about the crime itself.

Extrinsic evidence: In Virginia, extrinsic evidence of the conviction is only permitted if the witness is asked and denies being convicted. Under the federal rule, extrinsic evidence of a prior conviction is permitted regardless. In both jurisdictions, inquiry beyond the nature (i.e., name) of the conviction is generally prohibited, although some dispensation is provided to criminal defendants. "Under Virginia law, a criminal defendant whose testimony is impeached by evidence of a prior felony conviction has the right to introduce limited evidence to show that the prior conviction was obtained on the basis of perjured testimony." Reed v. Com., 6 Va. App. 65, 68, 366 S.E.2d 274, 276 (Va. App. 1988).

Other distinctions include that, in Virginia, juvenile convictions cannot in any circumstances be used to impeach a witness' character for truthfulness; there is no special allowance made for older convictions; or any explicit provision governing impeachment with convictions for which a pardon has been obtained. Sulton v. FedEx Ground Package System, 80 Va. Cir. 385 (Va. Cir. 2010) ("Virginia has no corollary to Federal Rule of Evidence Rule 609(c).") Virginia also provides that adverse witnesses called by a party cannot be impeached with prior convictions by that party. The federal rule is to the contrary. Fed. R. Ev. 607. The Virginia rule does not mention convictions pending appeal, but as with the federal rule, "the pendency of an appeal does not preclude use of a conviction for impeachment purposes." Peterson v. Com., 225 Va. 289, 297, 302

S.E.2d 520, 526 (1983).

Although not discussed in the rule, the United States Supreme Court has placed significant restrictions on criminal defendants seeking to appeal a trial court's impeachment ruling. To appeal, a criminal defendant must testify at trial, Luce v. U.S, 469 U.S. 38, 41 (1984), and cannot bring the impeachment out himself, Ohler v. U.S., 529 U.S. 753, 755-56 (2000). Although claims of error will be less frequent on appeal in Virginia, given the trial court's more limited discretion in weighing impeachment by prior conviction, decisions following *Luce* and *Ohler* appear in Virginia case law. See Reed v. Com., 6 Va. App. 65, 69, 366 S.E.2d 274, 277 (Va. App. 1988) ("Although *Luce* involved an interpretation of Federal Rule of Evidence 609 and was not of constitutional dimension, we find the analysis persuasive and we adopt its reasoning to apply to our rules of evidence."); Stevenson v. Com., 1210-05-1, 2006 WL 1459868 (Va. App. 2006) (unpublished) (citing *Ohler* in related context).

FED. R. EV. 610. RELIGIOUS BELIEFS OR OPINIONS

Evidence of a witness's religious beliefs or opinions is not admissible to attack or support the witness's credibility.

VA. R. EV. 2:610. BIAS OR PREJUDICE OF A WITNESS

A witness may be impeached by a showing that the witness is biased for or prejudiced against a party. Extrinsic evidence of such bias or prejudice may be admitted.

Comparison and Commentary

Rule 610 and Rule 2:610 have little in common apart from the general topic of witness credibility. The federal rule makes explicit that a witness' religious beliefs alone are not a permissible ground for impeaching that witness' credibility. Virginia leaves this to be handled by general relevance rules, which likely can handle the task.

Instead, Virginia uses Rule 610 to note that bias is a permissible form of impeachment (a proposition that would be uncontroversial without a rule), and that extrinsic evidence of bias can be introduced. This is to be contrasted with the rules regarding impeachment of a witness' character for truthfulness, where extrinsic evidence is generally not permitted. See Rule 2:608(b); Harrison v. Com., 56 Va. App. 382, 388, 694 S.E.2d 247, 250 (Va. App. 2010) (quoting Fourth Circuit case).

Fed. R. Ev. 611. Mode and Order of Examining Witnesses and Presenting Evidence

(a) Control by the Court; Purposes. The court should exercise reasonable control over the mode and order of examining witnesses and presenting evidence so as to:

> (1) make those procedures effective for determining the truth;

> (2) avoid wasting time; and

> (3) protect witnesses from harassment or undue embarrassment.

(b) Scope of Cross-Examination. Cross-examination should not go beyond the subject matter of the direct examination and matters affecting the witness's credibility. The court may allow inquiry into additional matters as if on direct examination.

(c) Leading Questions. Leading questions should not be used on direct examination except as necessary to develop the witness's testimony. Ordinarily, the court should allow leading questions:

> (1) on cross-examination; and

> (2) when a party calls a hostile witness, an adverse

party, or a witness identified with an adverse party.

VA. R. EV. 2:611. MODE AND ORDER OF INTERROGATION AND PRESENTATION (Rule 2:611(c) derived from Code § 8.01-401(A))

(a) Presentation of evidence. The mode and order of interrogating witnesses and presenting evidence may be determined by the court so as to (1) facilitate the ascertainment of the truth, (2) avoid needless consumption of time, and (3) protect witnesses from harassment or undue embarrassment.

(b) Scope of cross-examination.

(i) Cross-examination should be limited to the subject matter of the direct examination and matters affecting the credibility of the witness. The court may, in the exercise of discretion, permit inquiry into additional matters as if on direct examination.

(ii) In a criminal case, if a defendant testifies on his or her own behalf and denies guilt as to an offense charged, cross-examination of the defendant may be permitted in the discretion of the court into any matter relevant to the issue of guilt or innocence.

(c) Leading questions. Leading questions should not be used on the direct examination of a witness except as may be permitted by the court in its discretion to allow a party to develop the testimony. Leading questions should be permitted on cross-examination. Whenever a party calls a hostile witness, an adverse party, a witness having an adverse interest, or a witness proving adverse, interrogation may be by leading questions.

Comparison and Commentary

Both the Virginia and federal rules provide guidance to trial courts regarding the general presentation of testimony. The two provisions are essentially the same. The only textual deviation is that the Virginia rule states that cross-examination of a criminal defendant can go beyond the scope of the direct examination to encompass "any matter relevant to the issue of guilt or innocence." This provision answers a question raised in the Federal Advisory Committee Notes -- "the extent to which an accused who elects to testify thereby waives his privilege against self-incrimination" -- and specifically, whether the defendant can "foreclose inquiry into an aspect or element of the crime by avoiding it on direct?" The federal rule provides no answer, noting that it is a constitutional question and thus "ought not to be determined as a by-product of a rule on scope of cross-examination." Virginia's rule answers the question in the negative, both as an evidentiary and constitutional matter. Satcher v. Com., 244 Va. 220, 252, 421 S.E.2d 821, 840 (Va. 1992) ("When [the defendant] took the witness stand and denied complicity in the offenses then on trial, he opened the door for any questions on cross-examination that the trial court, in the exercise of its discretion, might find relevant to the issue of guilt or innocence."); Smith v. Com., 182 Va. 585, 597-98, 30 S.E.2d 26, 31 (Va. 1944) ("when the accused takes the stand in his own behalf he is not only subject to cross-examination, but 'absolutely and in all respects' waives his privilege against self-incrimination and is to be treated as any other witness"). In the federal system, the scope of direct more clearly governs the extent of cross-examination, even of a criminal defendant, but wide latitude is nevertheless provided. U.S. v. Vasquez, 858 F.2d 1387, 1392 (9th Cir. 1988) (rejecting defendant's contention that government's cross-examination went beyond the scope); U.S. v. Lara, 181 F.3d 183, 200 (1st Cir. 1999) (interpreting Rule 611 to vest trial court with discretion on the matter and after concluding that questions were within the scope, adding that "whether or not the questions [on cross of the defendant] fell within the scope of the direct examination, we could not say that the trial judge[] ... abuse[d its] discretion" in allowing them).

FED. R. EV. 612. WRITING USED TO REFRESH A WITNESS'S MEMORY

(a) Scope. This rule gives an adverse party certain options when a witness uses a writing to refresh memory:

>   **(1)** while testifying; or

>   **(2)** before testifying, if the court decides that justice requires the party to have those options.

(b) Adverse Party's Options; Deleting Unrelated Matter. Unless 18 U.S.C. § 3500 provides otherwise in a criminal case, an adverse party is entitled to have the writing produced at the hearing, to inspect it, to cross-examine the witness about it, and to introduce in evidence any portion that relates to the witness's testimony. If the producing party claims that the writing includes unrelated matter, the court must examine the writing in camera, delete any unrelated portion, and order that the rest be delivered to the adverse party. Any portion deleted over objection must be preserved for the record.

(c) Failure to Produce or Deliver the Writing. If a writing is not produced or is not delivered as ordered, the court may issue any appropriate order. But if the prosecution does not comply in a criminal case, the court must strike the witness's testimony or--if justice so requires--declare a mistrial.

VA. R. EV. 2:612. WRITING OR OBJECT USED TO REFRESH MEMORY

If while testifying, a witness uses a writing or object to refresh his memory, an adverse party is entitled to have the writing or object produced at the trial, hearing, or deposition in which the witness is testifying.

Comparison and Commentary

Witnesses commonly refer to documents to refresh their memory prior to or during trial. The federal and Virginia rules both provide that when witnesses do so during their testimony, the "adverse party" obtains the right to request that the memory-refreshing item be produced for examination. The rules diverge in two significant ways. First, the federal rule also extends to documents consulted by a witness "before testifying," while Virginia's rule does not. Although the Virginia case that makes this point most directly, leaves open the prospect that a trial court might nevertheless order the production. See McGann v. Com., 15 Va. App. 448, 452, 424 S.E.2d 706, 709 (Va. App. 1992) (finding no error in trial court's refusal to order production of notes reviewed by witness the morning of the trial, and noting that "the majority of jurisdictions have held that materials used by a witness before coming into the courtroom to testify in order to refresh his or her memory are not available for inspection by the opposing party unless the court in its discretion orders otherwise"). The second distinction concerns the use of the memory-refreshing item upon production. The federal rules state that in a criminal case, the adverse party can introduce into evidence "any portion [of the item] that relates to the witness's testimony." The Virginia rule only requires that the item be "produced at trial." In Virginia, admissibility or use in cross-examination remains subject to the general evidence rules. For example, the Codification Commentary to Rule 2:612 cites Acuar v. Letourneau, 260 Va. 180, 187, 531 S.E.2d 316, 320 (Va. 2000), which held that a trial court erred by permitting references to an accident report made inadmissible by statute, even though a witness testified to having used the report to refresh his recollection.

FED. R. EV. 613. WITNESS'S PRIOR STATEMENT

(a) Showing or Disclosing the Statement During Examination. When examining a witness about the witness's prior statement, a party need not show it or disclose its contents to the witness. But the party must, on request, show it or disclose its contents to an adverse party's attorney.

(b) Extrinsic Evidence of a Prior Inconsistent Statement. Extrinsic evidence of a witness's prior inconsistent statement is admissible only if the witness is given an opportunity to explain or deny the statement and an adverse party is given an opportunity to examine the witness about it, or if justice so requires. This subdivision (b) does not apply to an opposing party's statement under Rule 801(d)(2).

VA. R. EV. 2:613. PRIOR STATEMENTS OF WITNESS

(Rule 2:613(a)(i) derived from Code § 8.01-403; Rule 2:613(b)(i) derived from Code §§ 8.01-404 and 19.2-268.1; and Rule 2:613(b)(ii) derived from Code § 8.01-404)

(a) Examining witness concerning prior oral statement.

(i) Prior oral statements of witnesses. In examining a witness in any civil or criminal case concerning a prior oral statement, the circumstances of the supposed statement, sufficient to designate the particular occasion, must be mentioned to the witness, and the witness must be asked whether the statement was made.

(ii) Extrinsic evidence of prior inconsistent oral statement of witness. Extrinsic evidence of a prior inconsistent oral statement by a witness is not admissible unless the witness is first given an opportunity to explain or deny the statement and the opposing party is given an opportunity to interrogate the witness thereon, or the interests of justice otherwise require. This provision does not apply to admissions of a party opponent.

Extrinsic evidence of a witness' prior inconsistent statement is not admissible unless the witness denies or does not remember the prior inconsistent statement. Extrinsic evidence of collateral statements is not admissible.

(b) Contradiction by prior inconsistent writing.

(i) General rule. In any civil or criminal case, a witness may be cross-examined as to previous statements made by the witness in writing or reduced to writing, relating to the subject matter of the action, without such writing being shown to the witness; but if the intent is to contradict such witness by the writing, his or her attention must, before such contradictory proof can be given, be called to the particular occasion on which the writing is supposed to have been made; the witness may be asked whether he or she made a writing of the purport of the one to be offered, and if the witness denies making it, or does not admit its execution, it shall then be shown to the witness, and if the witness admits its genuineness, the witness shall be allowed to make an explanation of it; but the court may, at any time during the trial, require the production of the writing for its inspection, and the court may then make such use of it for the purpose of the trial as it may think best.

(ii) Personal Injury or Wrongful Death Cases. Notwithstanding the general principles stated in this subpart (b), in an action to recover for personal injury or wrongful death, no ex parte affidavit or statement in writing other than a deposition, after due notice, of a witness and no extrajudicial recording made at any time other than simultaneously with the wrongful act or negligence at issue of the voice of such witness, or reproduction or transcript thereof, as to the facts or circumstances attending the wrongful act or neglect complained of, shall be used to contradict such witness in the case. Nothing in this subdivision shall be construed to prohibit the use of any such ex parte affidavit or statement in an action on an insurance policy based upon a judgment recovered in a personal injury or wrongful death case.

Comparison and Commentary

The federal and Virginia rules differ on the procedural niceties required when a party attempts to use a testifying witness' prior statement at trial. The federal rule states that a party need not disclose the prior statement to the witness, but must show the statement, upon request, to the adverse attorney. The Virginia rule, by contrast, states that the witness must be informed of the circumstances of the statement and be asked whether it was made.

The rules also discuss when the statement can be proven by extrinsic evidence. The Virginia rule does not permit extrinsic evidence if the witness acknowledges having made the statement, and bars extrinsic evidence of "collateral" statements. These provisions are not included in the federal rule; the federal rules leave questions about undue "collateral-ness" to Rule 403. When extrinsic evidence is introduced, both the Virginia and federal rules, in almost identical language, require that the witness be given an opportunity to opine on the prior statement, and the adverse party be given an opportunity to examine the witness regarding it. The Virginia rule includes a critical "first" ("the witness is **first** given an opportunity to explain or deny the statement"), which clarifies a point that has led to a federal circuit split. See Katharine T. Schaffzin, *Sweet Caroline: The Backslide from Federal Rule of Evidence 613(b) to the Rule in Queen Caroline's Case*, 47 U. Mich. J.L. Reform 283, 300 (2014) (describing split). Under the Virginia rule, the witness must be asked to explain the statement before extrinsic evidence of the statement is offered. The majority of the federal circuits, however, permit extrinsic evidence as long as an opportunity exists, at some point, for the other party to ask the witness about the statement. Id. at 301 ("Where the witness remained available for recall, [most federal] courts have admitted evidence of a witness's prior inconsistent statements that the proponent introduced after the court had excused the witness.")

Both rules except opposing party statements from any such requirements, although the Virginia rule labels such statements "admissions of a party opponent" – while surely simply meaning any statement of a party offered by the opposing party as in Rule 2:803(0).

The federal rule has no parallel to Virginia's Rule 2:613(b). Rule 2:613(b)(i) is unexceptional. It applies to written statements of a testifying witness (written by the witness or by someone else on the witness' behalf), allowing cross-examination on such writings, of course, and providing a series of logistical requirements that are generally consistent with part (a) of the rule.

Virginia Rule 2:613(b)(ii) is quite extraordinary. It precludes the use of a witness' written or recorded statements (other than a deposition) to contradict that witness' testimony in a personal injury (or death) lawsuit. The Virginia Supreme Court has explained the rule's purpose as follows:

> "The purpose of [the statutory precursor to Rule 2:613(b)(ii)] was to correct an unfair practice which had developed, by which claim adjusters would hasten to the scene of an accident and obtain written statements from all eye-witnesses. Frequently, these statements were neither full nor correct and were signed by persons who had not fully recovered from shock and hence were not in full possession of their faculties. Later, such persons, when testifying as witnesses, would be confronted with their signed statements and, after admitting their signatures, these

statements would be introduced in evidence as impeachment of their testimony given on the witness stand." Harris v. Harrington, 180 Va. 210, 220, 22 S.E.2d 13, 17 (Va. 1942).

The Virginia Supreme Court has endeavored to narrowly construe this unusual statutory prohibition. Excludable, contradicting statement are only those "of [the] witness," which generally means that for writings, "the written document was either signed by the witness or in the handwriting of the witness." Scott v. Greater Richmond Transit Co., 241 Va. 300, 303, 402 S.E.2d 214, 217 (Va. 1991). With respect to recordings, witnesses can still be contradicted with oral statements even if those statements happen to be recorded, as long as the recording itself is not used. Ruhlin v. Samaan, 282 Va. 371, 379-80, 718 S.E.2d 447, 451 (Va. 2011) (impeachment with oral content of phone calls recorded by insurance company). And the recorded statement can be used for a purpose such as refreshing a witness' recollection, since refreshing is not contradicting. Id. In addition, recorded statements of likely witnesses can be introduced (assuming admissibility) before the witness has testified, since in such circumstances the statements are not (yet) offered to "contradict." Gray v. Rhoads, 268 Va. 81, 88-89, 597 S.E.2d 93, 98 (Va. 2004).

Virginia law also includes a statute that prohibits the introduction of recorded telephone conversations in civil cases, except if both parties were aware that the conversation was being recorded, or "the portion of the recording to be admitted contains admissions that, if true, would constitute criminal conduct which is the basis for the civil action, and one of the parties was aware of the recording and the proceeding is not one for divorce, separate maintenance or annulment of a marriage." Va. Code § 8.01-420.2; see also 18 U.S.C. § 2511 (federal wiretapping statute). Both the federal and Virginia statutes include numerous exceptions.

FED. R. EV. 614. COURT'S CALLING OR EXAMINING A WITNESS

(a) Calling. The court may call a witness on its own or at a party's request. Each party is entitled to cross-examine the witness.

(b) Examining. The court may examine a witness regardless of who calls the witness.

(c) Objections. A party may object to the court's calling or examining a witness either at that time or at the next opportunity when the jury is not present.

VA. R. EV. 2:614. CALLING AND INTERROGATION OF WITNESSES BY COURT

(a) Calling by the court in civil cases. The court, on motion of a party or on its own motion, may call witnesses, and all parties are entitled to cross-examine. The calling of a witness by the court is a matter resting in the trial judge's sound discretion and should be exercised with great care.

(b) Interrogation by the court. In a civil or criminal case, the court may question witnesses, whether called by itself or a party, subject to the applicable Rules of Evidence.

Comparison and Commentary

The federal and Virginia rules provide that judges may call witnesses and question those witnesses, as well as the witnesses called by the parties. The federal rule applies in civil and criminal cases. The Virginia rule with respect to calling witnesses appears to apply, by its title, only to civil cases. See Codification Commentary to Rule 2:614 ("Virginia reported case law is silent on the topic of the judge calling witnesses in criminal cases.") As reflected in the case cited on this point in the Comparison and Commentary to Rule 2:607, the case law does not make such a clear civil-criminal distinction. In addition, Virginia's byzantine restrictions on impeaching one's own witness make this rule particularly attractive to an attorney considering calling a potentially hostile witness. For if the judge calls the witness, the rule allows "all parties" to cross-examine the witness and presumably to impeach her as well. See Rule 2:607.

FED. R. EV. 615. EXCLUDING WITNESSES

At a party's request, the court must order witnesses excluded so that they cannot hear other witnesses' testimony. Or the court may do so on its own. But this rule does not authorize excluding:

(a) a party who is a natural person;

(b) an officer or employee of a party that is not a natural person, after being designated as the party's representative by its attorney;

(c) a person whose presence a party shows to be essential to presenting the party's claim or defense; or

(d) a person authorized by statute to be present.

VA. R. EV. 2:615. EXCLUSION OF WITNESSES (Rule 2:615(a) derived from Code §§ 8.01-375, 19.2-184, and 19.2-265.1; Rule 2:615(b) derived from Code § 8.01-375; and Rule 2:615(c) derived from Code § 19.2-265.1)

(a) The court, in a civil or criminal case, may on its own motion and shall on the motion of any party, require the exclusion of every witness including, but not limited to, police officers or other investigators. The court may also order that each excluded witness be kept separate from all other witnesses. But each named party who is an individual, one officer or agent of each party which is a corporation, limited liability entity or association, and an attorney alleged in a habeas corpus proceeding to have acted ineffectively shall be exempt from the exclusion as a matter of right.

(b) Where expert witnesses are to testify in the case, the court may, at the request of all parties, allow one expert witness for each party to remain in the courtroom; however, in cases pertaining to the distribution of marital property pursuant to § 20-107.3 or the determination of child or spousal support pursuant to § 20-108.1, the court may, upon motion of any party, allow one expert witness for each party to remain in the courtroom throughout the hearing.

(c) Any victim as defined in Code § 19.2-11.01 who is to be called as a witness may remain in the courtroom and shall not be excluded unless pursuant to Code § 19.2-265.01 the court determines, in its discretion, that the presence of the victim would impair the conduct of a fair trial.

Comparison and Commentary

The federal and Virginia rules grant the trial court discretion to exclude witnesses from the proceedings so as to limit contamination of the witness' potential testimony. U.S. v. Collins, 340 F.3d 672, 681 (8th Cir. 2003) ("The purpose of sequestration is to prevent witnesses from tailoring their testimony to that of prior witnesses and to aid in detection of dishonesty.") Individual ("natural") parties are excepted in both rules, of course, as is a single representative of a non-human entity (e.g., a corporation). The Virginia rule also allows an attorney claimed to have been constitutionally ineffective to attend a habeas proceeding.

The Virginia rule does not adopt the common federal practice of allowing a testifying "case agent" to remain with the prosecuting attorney throughout the trial. See U.S. v. Gonzalez, 918 F.2d 1129,

1138 (3d Cir. 1990) (noting that "[m]any circuits recognize a 'case agent' exception to the typical rule of sequestration," under Rule 615(b) and that "these cases hold that the government case agent responsible for a particular investigation should be permitted to remain in the courtroom, even though the agent will often testify later on behalf of the government"); U.S. v. Kosko, 870 F.2d 162, 164 (4th Cir. 1989) ("Ordinarily, when a sequestration rule is invoked, the government may be permitted to have only one case agent in the courtroom during trial."). Virginia's rule specifically mentions "police officers" among those who "shall" be excluded, and allows a representative only of "a party which is a corporation, limited liability entity or association."

The Virginia rule also provides the court with explicit authority to order the witnesses to be kept separate from each other, a provision that is absent from the federal rule. U.S. v. Rhynes, 218 F.3d 310, 316 (4th Cir. 2000) (rejecting contention that invocation of Rule 615 prevented lawyer from discussing witness testimony with another witness as the "Rule's plain language relates only to 'witnesses,' and it serves only to exclude witnesses from the courtroom"). Nevertheless, the federal courts assume the power to include such provisions in Rule 615 sequestration orders. U.S. v. Walker, 613 F.2d 1349, 1354 (5th Cir. 1980) ("Sequestration requires that witnesses not discuss the case among themselves or anyone else, other than the counsel for the parties."); U.S. v. Jenkins, 178 F.3d 1287 (4th Cir. 1999) (noting that "[b]efore trial, the district court entered a sequestration order pursuant to Federal Rule of Evidence 615, under which all witnesses were excluded from the court room and were expressly forbidden from discussing their testimony with each other").

ARTICLE VII. OPINIONS AND EXPERT TESTIMONY

FED. R. EV. 701. OPINION TESTIMONY BY LAY WITNESSES

If a witness is not testifying as an expert, testimony in the form of an opinion is limited to one that is:

(a) rationally based on the witness's perception;

(b) helpful to clearly understanding the witness's testimony or to determining a fact in issue; and

(c) not based on scientific, technical, or other specialized knowledge within the scope of Rule 702.

VA. R. EV. 2:701. OPINION TESTIMONY BY LAY WITNESSES (derived from Code § 8.01-401.3(B))

Opinion testimony by a lay witness is admissible if it is reasonably based upon the personal experience or observations of the witness and will aid the trier of fact in understanding the witness' perceptions. Lay opinion may relate to any matter, such as--but not limited to--sanity, capacity, physical condition or disability, speed of a vehicle, the value of property, identity, causation, time, the meaning of words, similarity of objects, handwriting, visibility or the general physical situation at a particular location. However, lay witness testimony that amounts only to an opinion of law is inadmissible.

Comparison and Commentary

The Virginia and federal rules permit opinion testimony by lay witnesses under similar conditions. The testimony must be based on the witness' perceptions and must aid the trier of fact. Federal courts interpret the rule to liberally allow lay witness opinions about age, drunkenness, etc., because such testimony adds to testimony about underlying perceptions, but exclude opinions that are conclusory and add nothing to the underlying facts. Virginia law is similar. See Harman v. Honeywell Int'l, 758 S.E.2d 515, 524 (Va. 2014) ("if the witness can conveniently relate the facts in a manner that will provide the jury with an adequate understanding of the issue, the witness's opinion based on those facts is unnecessary and therefore inadmissible," but where lay witness's "statements that the Mooney plane was … more complex, and more difficult to maneuver than the Cessna plane aided the jury" they constituted "proper lay opinion testimony pursuant to Rule 2:701"). Rule 2:701 departs from the federal rule by providing a series of examples of permitted lay opinion testimony.

Virginia case law, like that in the federal courts, permits a non-expert's specialized testimony in certain circumstances. See Snyder Plaza Properties v. Adams Outdoor Adver., 259 Va. 635, 644, 528 S.E.2d 452, 458 (2000) ("We have recognized the general rule that an owner of property is competent and qualified to render a lay opinion regarding the value of that property."); Advisory Committee Note to Fed. R. Ev. 701.

Both the federal rules (generally) and the Virginia evidence code (in civil cases) eliminate the common law's prohibition of testimony on "ultimate" issues (see Rule 704), while excluding conclusory assertions of liability under Rules 701 and 702 as not helpful to the trier of fact. See Advisory Committee Note to Fed. R. Ev. 704. Virginia rule 2:701 also makes lay opinion testimony about the law inadmissible – something the federal courts accomplish by simply deeming such testimony "unhelpful."

Virginia Rule 2:701 does not include the federal rule's warning (added by amendment in 2000) that lay opinion testimony cannot be based on scientific, technical or specialized knowledge. The federal amendment was intended to ensure that the expert testimony requirements in Rule 702 could not be "evaded through the simple expedient of proffering an expert in lay witness clothing." Advisory Committee Note to 2000 Amendment to Fed. R. Ev. 701. Virginia courts police this same boundary even though Rule 2:701 does not make the boundary as explicit. White v. Com., 46 Va. App. 123, 132, 616 S.E.2d 49, 53 (2005) aff'd, 272 Va. 619, 636 S.E.2d 353 (2006) (upholding exclusion of testimony on defendant's sanity where witness was not qualified as an expert).

FED. R. EV. 702. TESTIMONY BY EXPERT WITNESSES

A witness who is qualified as an expert by knowledge, skill, experience, training, or education may testify in the form of an opinion or otherwise if:

(a) the expert's scientific, technical, or other specialized knowledge will help the trier of fact to understand the evidence or to determine a fact in issue;

(b) the testimony is based on sufficient facts or data;

(c) the testimony is the product of reliable principles and methods; and

(d) the expert has reliably applied the principles and methods to the facts of the case.

VA. R. EV. 2:702. TESTIMONY BY EXPERTS (Rule 2:702(a)(i) derived from Code § 8.01-401.3(A))

(a) Use of Expert Testimony.

(i) In a civil proceeding, if scientific, technical, or other specialized knowledge will assist the trier of fact to understand the evidence or to determine a fact in issue, a witness qualified as an expert by knowledge, skill, experience, training, or education may testify thereto in the form of an opinion or otherwise.

(ii) In a criminal proceeding, expert testimony is admissible if the standards set forth in subdivision (a)(i) of this Rule are met and, in addition, the court finds that the subject matter is beyond the knowledge and experience of ordinary persons, such that the jury needs expert opinion in order to comprehend the subject matter, form an intelligent opinion, and draw its conclusions.

(b) Form of Opinion. Expert testimony may include opinions of the witness established with a reasonable degree of probability, or it may address empirical data from which such probability may be established in the mind of the finder of fact. Testimony that is speculative, or which opines on the credibility of another witness, is not admissible.

Comparison and Commentary

Unlike the federal rule, Virginia Rule 2:702, based in part on a statutory provision specific to civil cases, contains distinct subdivisions governing expert testimony in civil and criminal cases. The Virginia rule also includes a subsection discussing the "form" that expert opinion testimony can take. As explained below, while Virginia's rule thus differs from its federal counterpart, the distinctions are largely superficial.

Rule 2:702(a)(i) is identical to the pre-2000 Federal Rule 702. The federal rule was amended in 2000 in the wake of Supreme Court decisions interpreting then-existing Rule 702, Daubert v. Merrell Dow Pharmaceuticals, 509 U.S. 579 (1993) and Kumho Tire v. Carmichael, 526 U.S. 137 (1999). The current federal rule explicitly incorporates the "reliability" and "gatekeeper" principles articulated in *Daubert* and *Kumho Tire*, while the Virginia rule does so only (as the pre-2000 federal rule did) implicitly. The Virginia courts have, in fact, explicitly left open the question of the direct application of *Daubert* in Virginia, although the Virginia Supreme Court has indicated approval of the federal case. See John v. Im, 263 Va. 315, 322 & n.3, 559 S.E.2d 694, 698 & n.3 (2002). That Court has also rejected invitations to adopt *Daubert*'s principal rival, the *Frye* test. Spencer v. Com., 238 Va. 563, 573 & n.5, 385 S.E.2d 850, 856 & n.5 (1989) ("We have rejected the adoption of the *Frye* test."); O'Dell v. Com., 234 Va. 672, 696, 364 S.E.2d 491, 504 (1988) (same).

Labels aside, Virginia courts, like federal courts, assess expert testimony for reliability. "Expert testimony is inadmissible if it is speculative or founded on assumptions that have an insufficient factual basis" of if the "expert has failed to consider all variables bearing on the inferences to be drawn from the facts observed." *Im* at 320; Satcher v. Com., 244 Va. 220, 241, 421 S.E.2d 821, 834 (1992) (endorsing trial court's screening of expert testimony for "reliab[ility]"); Hasson v. Com., 2006 WL 1387974, at *10 (Va. Ct. App. 2006) (unpublished) ("while not dispositive as a test in Virginia, the *Daubert* discussion concerning the factors that comprise an analysis of scientific reliability certainly is instructive").

Rule 2:702(a)(ii) supplements the requirements for admission of expert testimony in criminal cases. The requirement added by this subsection appears to simply elaborate on Rule 2:702(a)(i)'s command (also present in the federal rule) that the expert testimony "assist the trier of fact." Thus, it is not clear that Rule 2:702 truly creates separate standards for the admission of expert testimony in civil and criminal trials. See, e.g., Nichols v. Com., 6 Va. App. 426, 430-31, 369 S.E.2d 218, 220-21 (1988) (expert testimony "'is admissible not only when scientific knowledge is required, but when experience and observation in a special calling give the expert knowledge of a subject beyond that of persons of common intelligence and ordinary experience,'" but "inadmissible on matters of common knowledge or those as to which the jury are as competent to form an intelligent and accurate opinion as the witness"); Velazquez v. Com., 263 Va. 95, 103, 557 S.E.2d 213, 218 (2002) ("The sole purpose of permitting expert testimony is to assist the trier of fact to understand the evidence presented or to determine a fact in issue.")

A trial court's decision in Virginia, as in the federal system, with regard to whether to admit expert testimony is reviewed under the deferential abuse of discretion standard. John v. Im, 263 Va. 315, 320, 559 S.E.2d 694, 696 (2002); Gen. Elec. Co. v. Joiner, 522 U.S. 136, 146 (1997) ("abuse of discretion is the proper standard by which to review a district court's decision to admit or exclude scientific evidence").

Rule 2:702 deviates from the federal rule in its inclusion of subsection (b), which governs the form of permissible expert testimony. The provision limits such testimony to expert opinions based on a "reasonable degree of probability." As applied in Virginia, this provision seems to mean only that the expert's testimony cannot be speculative, an uncontroversial point that is likely unnecessary since it is covered by other portions of the rules. See Spruill v. Com., 221 Va. 475, 479, 271 S.E.2d 419, 421 (1980) ("A medical opinion based on a 'possibility' is irrelevant, purely speculative and, hence, inadmissible. In order for such testimony to become relevant, it must be brought out of the realm of speculation and into the realm of reasonable probability; the law in this area deals in 'probabilities' and not 'possibilities.'"); Cantrell v. Com., 229 Va. 387, 396, 329 S.E.2d 22, 28 (1985) (rejecting Commonwealth's argument that defense expert's testimony was properly excluded because it purportedly "dealt only with possibilities, rather than reasonable probabilities"). Piling on, subsection (b) explicitly prohibits testimony that is "speculative."

Rule 2:702(b), applicable both to civil and criminal cases, also states that the expert can testify to "empirical data" underlying a conclusion. This provision likely comes from Cantrell v. Com., where the Virginia Supreme Court endorsed defense expert testimony that referenced "empirical data available in the discipline of pathology" – specifically, instances of other head injuries investigated by the testifying expert – in presenting his conclusions to the jury. *Cantrell* at 396. A curiosity about *Cantrell*, however, is that the Court there relied on Va. Code § 8.01-401.1 to reach its conclusion that the expert testimony was proper, even though that section applies, by its terms, to "any civil action" and *Cantrell* was a criminal case.

Subsection (b) also bars expert testimony that "opines on the credibility of another witness." Cf. James v. Com., 254 Va. 95, 98, 487 S.E.2d 205, 207 (1997) ("the credibility of witnesses and the weight to be given to their testimony are questions exclusively for the jury"). This prohibition echoes one established in federal court through case law interpreting the "assist the trier of fact" requirement as well as Rule 403. United States v. Toledo, 985 F.2d 1462, 1470 (10th Cir. 1993) ("The credibility of witnesses is generally not an appropriate subject for expert testimony.... Such testimony is often excluded because it is not helpful to the jury, which can make its own determination of credibility.") The prohibition in the federal courts does not bar experts, such as those testifying about flaws in the accuracy of eyewitness identifications, from testifying about factors that might influence the credibility of another witness. Subsection (b) of the Virginia rule should be interpreted in similar fashion. That said, Rule 2:702(b)'s explicit and unqualified command may cause Virginia courts to react more negatively to the admission of testimony that touches on witness credibility. This may explain the Virginia courts' skepticism toward the admissibility of eyewitness identification expert testimony, despite a national trend toward growing acceptance. Compare Rodriguez v. Com., 20 Va. App. 122, 128, 455 S.E.2d 724, 727 (1995) (expressing reluctance to admit eyewitness expert testimony) with State v. Guilbert, 49 A.3d 705, 720 (Conn. 2012) (noting "widespread judicial recognition" of value of such testimony in reversing *Rodriguez*–like precedent).

A statute outside the evidence code governs the requisite qualifications for expert testimony on the "standard of care" in medical malpractice cases. See V.A. Code § 8.01-581.20 (medical malpractice); Perdieu v. Blackstone Family Practice Ctr., 264 Va. 408, 419, 568 S.E.2d 703, 709 (2002) ("the requirements of Code §8.01-581.20 are mandatory"). Virginia also includes a specific statutory provision governing expert testimony by chiropractors and physician assistants. Va. Code § 8.01-401.2.

Fed. R. Ev. 703. Bases of an Expert's Opinion Testimony

An expert may base an opinion on facts or data in the case that the expert has been made aware of or personally observed. If experts in the particular field would reasonably rely on those kinds of facts or data in forming an opinion on the subject, they need not be admissible for the opinion to be admitted. But if the facts or data would otherwise be inadmissible, the proponent of the opinion may disclose them to the jury only if their probative value in helping the jury evaluate the opinion substantially outweighs their prejudicial effect.

Va. R. Ev. 2:703. Basis Of Expert Testimony (Rule 2:703(a) derived from Code § 8.01-401.1)

(a) Civil Cases. In a civil action an expert witness may give testimony and render an opinion or draw inferences from facts, circumstances, or data made known to or perceived by such witness at or before the hearing or trial during which the witness is called upon to testify. The facts, circumstances, or data relied upon by such witness in forming an opinion or drawing inferences, if of a type normally relied upon by others in the particular field of expertise in forming opinions and drawing inferences, need not be admissible in evidence.

(b) Criminal Cases. In criminal cases, the opinion of an expert is generally admissible if it is based upon facts personally known or observed by the expert, or based upon facts in evidence.

Comparison and Commentary

Virginia again departs structurally from the federal rules in creating separate provisions for civil and criminal cases in its version of Rule 703. As with Rule 2:702, the separation results from the rule's derivation, in part, from a Virginia Code provision specific to civil cases, Va. Code § 8.01-401.1.

Virginia's Rule 2:703(a), applicable to civil cases, mirrors federal rule 703, with one exception. See Simpson v. Com., 227 Va. 557, 566, 318 S.E.2d 386, 391(1984) (explaining that § 8.01–401.1 "essentially adopts [Rule 703] of the Federal Rules of Evidence"). The federal rule was amended in 2003 to include a balancing test that determines when the expert can, during direct examination, disclose otherwise inadmissible information that the expert considered. The Virginia rule is silent on the question and the case law is generally hostile to revelation of inadmissible information solely to explain the basis of an expert's opinion. Lawrence v. Com., 279 Va. 490, 497, 689 S.E.2d 748, 752 (2010) (concluding that expert's testimony in Sexually Violent Predator Act proceeding impermissibly included hearsay regarding other misconduct that could not, through a limiting instruction, "effectively be restricted to proper use or purposes in the minds of the jury"); Com. v. Wynn, 277 Va. 92, 98, 100, 671 S.E.2d 137, 140 (2009) (reaching same conclusion while "apply[ing] the general rules applicable to expert testimony in other civil cases").

Virginia's Rule 2:703(b) governs criminal proceedings and departs drastically from Federal Rule 703, retaining the State's "historic restrictions upon expert testimony in criminal cases." Simpson, 227 Va. at 566 (1984) (rejecting argument to import federal standard in criminal cases). These historic restrictions only allow "[a]n expert [to] give an opinion based upon his own knowledge of facts" or "upon facts in evidence assumed in a hypothetical question." Walrod v. Matthews, 210 Va. 382, 388, 171 S.E.2d 180, 185 (1969) (quoted in *Simpson*, supra); Davison v. Com., 18 Va. App. 496, 503, 445 S.E.2d 683, 687 (1994) (expert testifying in criminal trial can testify to an opinion based on facts personally known or facts in the form of a hypothetical question).

FED. R. EV. 704. OPINION ON AN ULTIMATE ISSUE

(a) In General--Not Automatically Objectionable. An opinion is not objectionable just because it embraces an ultimate issue.

(b) Exception. In a criminal case, an expert witness must not state an opinion about whether the defendant did or did not have a mental state or condition that constitutes an element of the crime charged or of a defense. Those matters are for the trier of fact alone.

VA. R. EV. 2:704. OPINION ON ULTIMATE ISSUE (Rule 2:704(a) derived from Code § 8.01-401.3(B) and (C))

(a) Civil Cases. In civil cases, no expert or lay witness shall be prohibited from expressing an otherwise admissible opinion or conclusion as to any matter of fact solely because that fact is the ultimate issue or critical to the resolution of the case. But in no event shall such witness be permitted to express any opinion which constitutes a conclusion of law. Any other exceptions to the "ultimate fact in issue" rule recognized in the Commonwealth remain in full force.

(b) Criminal Cases. In criminal proceedings, opinion testimony on the ultimate issues of fact is not admissible. This Rule does not require exclusion of otherwise proper expert testimony concerning a witness' or the defendant's mental disorder and the hypothetical effect of that disorder on a person in the witness' or the defendant's situation.

Comparison and Commentary

Virginia again structures its version of Rule 704 with separate sections dealing with civil and criminal cases. As with Rules 2:701 and 2:702, the separation results from the rule's derivation, in part, from a Virginia Code provision specific to civil cases, Va. Code § 8.01-401.3.

In civil cases, Virginia's Rule 2:704(a) mirrors federal rule 704(a), eliminating the common law bar to witness testimony that embraces the "ultimate issue" in the case. As under federal law, however, opinions that merely state a conclusion relevant to (or determinative of) the legal outcome can be excluded in Virginia because they are not helpful to the jury under Rules 2:701 and 2:702. As the Virginia Supreme Court has explained: "An expert's opinion is inadmissible,..., if it relates to matters about which the fact finder is equally as capable as the expert of reaching an intelligent and informed opinion." David A. Parker Enterprises v. Templeton, 251 Va. 235, 237, 467 S.E.2d 488, 490 (1996).

Virginia's rule also forbids testimony that constitutes "a conclusion of law," a result that, again, can be reached in the federal system on the ground that such a conclusion does not "help" the jury as required under Rule 702 or is unfairly prejudicial under Rule 403. See Hygh v. Jacobs, 961 F.2d 359, 363 (2d Cir. 1992) ("This circuit is in accord with other circuits in requiring exclusion of expert testimony that expresses a legal conclusion.")

Subdivision 2:704(b) addresses criminal cases in Virginia and purports, unlike subdivision (a), to bar testimony on the "ultimate issue." See, e.g., Jackson v. Com., 266 Va. 423, 438, 587 S.E.2d 532, 544 (2003) (expert could not opine as to whether defendant's confession was "false"). As discussed in the preceding paragraph this type of testimony is often excluded without an explicit prohibition, on the ground that it is not helpful to the jury. See Advisory Committee Note to Fed. R. Evid. 704 ("Under Rules 701 and 702, opinions must be helpful to the trier of fact, and Rule 403 provides for exclusion of evidence which wastes time. These provisions afford ample assurances against the admission of opinions which would merely tell the jury what result to reach, ...") As a consequence, subdivision (b) does not create as distinct a separation between Virginia civil and criminal evidence law as the text of Rule 2:704(b) might suggest. Further, the distinction between testimony that leads to an ultimate conclusion and testimony "on the ultimate conclusion" is a difficult one to draw. Id. (describing common-law rule barring ultimate opinion testimony as "unduly restrictive, difficult of application, and generally serv[ing] only to deprive the trier of fact of useful information"). For example, the Virginia Supreme Court has allowed testimony that constituted two thirds, but not the entirety, of the ultimate legal question:

> "The ultimate issue of fact before the jury was whether the pictures were 'obscene for children.' Whether the pictures appealed to prurient interest and whether the pictures had any socially redeeming value [ed. -- both testified to by the expert] were only two of the three subparts of the statutory test of material 'obscene for children.' Hence, considered individually or collectively, the expert's opinions did not invade the jury's right to resolve the ultimate issue of fact." Freeman v. Com., 223 Va. 301, 315, 288 S.E.2d 461, 468 (1982).

Difficulty of application notwithstanding, subdivision (b) gives criminal practitioners a firm basis on which to keep experts from testifying to conclusions that parallel the requisite legal findings in a case. Instead, experts may be required to testify only as to the underlying principles and findings from which the ultimate conclusion could be drawn, leaving the ultimate conclusion to the jury. Justiss v. Com., 61 Va. App. 261, 274, 734 S.E.2d 699, 705 (2012) (reversing conviction based on improper admission of detective's testimony that a BB gun could "cause serious bodily injury" where the testimony paralleled the legal question in the case).

The United States Congress added subsection (b) to Federal Rule 704 in response to a not guilty by reason of insanity verdict in the trial that followed the attempted murder of former President Reagan. U.S. v. Campos, 217 F.3d 707, 710 & n.1 (9th Cir. 2000). "While Congress primarily targeted subdivision (b) towards limiting the use of psychiatric expert testimony on whether a defendant is sane or insane," the federal courts have held "that Rule 704(b) is not limited in 'its reach to psychiatrists and other mental health experts,' but rather, extends to all expert witnesses." Id. at 711. This specific prohibition of expert testimony on a defendant's mental state that constitutes an element of an offense is absent from the Virginia rules. It would seem to be subsumed in Virginia's general prohibition of expert testimony on ultimate issues in criminal cases. However, the Virginia rules appear to specifically countenance some manner of testimony prohibited by the federal rule, in the final sentence of Rule 2:704(b). Fitzgerald v. Com., 223 Va. 615, 629, 292 S.E.2d 798, 806 (1982) (noting without disapproval that "the expert expressed his opinion that the ingestion of various quantities of LSD, Tranxene, and beer could not ... render a person incapable of having the intent to commit [certain criminal] acts"). That said, the specific case from which the last sentence of Rule 2:704(b) is drawn can be read more narrowly. See Pritchett v. Com., 263 Va. 182, 187, 557 S.E.2d 205, 208 (2002) (ruling that expert testimony about the reliability of a defendant's confession was permissible because "an expert may testify to a witness's or defendant's mental disorder and the hypothetical effect of that disorder on a person in the witness's or defendant's situation, so long as the expert does not opine on the truth of the statement at issue").

FED. R. EV. 705. DISCLOSING THE FACTS OR DATA UNDERLYING AN EXPERT'S OPINION

Unless the court orders otherwise, an expert may state an opinion--and give the reasons for it--without first testifying to the underlying facts or data. But the expert may be required to disclose those facts or data on cross-examination.

VA. R. EV. 2:705. FACTS OR DATA USED IN TESTIMONY (Rule 2:705(a) derived from Code § 8.01-401.1)

(a) Civil cases. In civil cases, an expert may testify in terms of opinion or inference and give reasons therefor without prior disclosure of the underlying facts or data, unless the court requires otherwise. The expert may in any event be required to disclose the underlying facts or data on cross-examination.

(b) Criminal cases. In criminal cases, the facts on which an expert may give an opinion shall be disclosed in the expert's testimony, or set forth in a hypothetical question.

Comparison and Commentary

Both the Virginia and federal rules allow experts in civil cases to testify as to their opinion without first specifying the underlying facts or data upon which the opinion is based. See Va. Code § 8.01-401.1. The federal rules apply this same rule in civil and criminal cases. Virginia's rule 2:705(b) distinguishes criminal cases, requiring experts in such cases to disclose the facts upon which an opinion is based at the same time as the opinion is expressed. A common way of doing so, referenced in the rule, is to cast the opinion as a response to a hypothetical factual scenario. Rule 2:705 follows from the division between expert testimony in civil and criminal cases in Virginia Rule 2:703. When an expert does testify to an opinion without first disclosing the facts upon which it is based, the adverse party can, of course, elicit those facts in cross-examination.

FED. R. EV. 706. COURT-APPOINTED EXPERT WITNESSES

(a) Appointment Process. On a party's motion or on its own, the court may order the parties to show cause why expert witnesses should not be appointed and may ask the parties to submit nominations. The court may appoint any expert that the parties agree on and any of its own choosing. But the court may only appoint someone who consents to act.

(b) Expert's Role. The court must inform the expert of the expert's duties. The court may do so in writing and have a copy filed with the clerk or may do so orally at a conference in which the parties have an opportunity to participate. The expert:

> **(1)** must advise the parties of any findings the expert makes;
>
> **(2)** may be deposed by any party;
>
> **(3)** may be called to testify by the court or any party; and
>
> **(4)** may be cross-examined by any party, including the party that called the expert.

(c) Compensation. The expert is entitled to a reasonable compensation, as set by the court. The compensation is payable as follows:

> **(1)** in a criminal case or in a civil case involving just compensation under the Fifth Amendment, from any funds that are provided by law; and
>
> **(2)** in any other civil case, by the parties in the proportion and at the time that the court directs--and the compensation is then charged like other costs.

(d) Disclosing the Appointment to the Jury. The court may authorize disclosure to the jury that the court appointed the expert.

(e) Parties' Choice of Their Own Experts. This rule does not limit a party in calling its own experts.

VA. R. EV. 706. USE OF LEARNED TREATISES WITH EXPERTS (Rule 2:706(a) derived from Code § 8.01-401.1)

[ed.- See Comparison and Commentary to Fed. R. Ev. 803(18).]

Comparison and Commentary

The federal rules contain a provision authorizing a court to appoint its own expert witness. Neither the Virginia rules nor Virginia case law contain any such provision. Related, but distinct from this concept, Virginia courts must, in some circumstances, appoint experts to assist criminal defendants at the Commonwealth's expense. Husske v. Com., 252 Va. 203, 211, 476 S.E.2d 920, 925 (Va. 1996); Va. Code § 19.2-168.1 (providing for court-appointed expert when the defense presents an insanity defense).

Virginia uses the number 2:706 for its discussion of the admissibility of learned treatises in conjunction with expert testimony. For the text of the Virginia rule and comparison to its federal analogue, see Fed. R. Ev. 803(18).

ARTICLE VIII. HEARSAY

RULE 801, EDITOR'S INTRODUCTORY NOTE

Federal Rule 801 includes a definition of hearsay, an exception for certain statements of testifying witnesses, and an exception for certain party opponent statements. Virginia's Rule 801 is similar, but distinct in important ways. Consequently, the federal rule is broken up below so that each of its three components can be compared to the analogous Virginia provisions.

Hearsay Definition

FED. R. EV. 801. DEFINITIONS THAT APPLY TO THIS ARTICLE; EXCLUSIONS FROM HEARSAY

(a) Statement. "Statement" means a person's oral assertion, written assertion, or nonverbal conduct, if the person intended it as an assertion.

(b) Declarant. "Declarant" means the person who made the statement.

(c) Hearsay. "Hearsay" means a statement that:

> (1) the declarant does not make while testifying at the current trial or hearing; and

> (2) a party offers in evidence to prove the truth of the matter asserted in the statement.

....

VA. R. EV. 2:801. DEFINITIONS

The following definitions apply under this article:

> (a) Statement. A "statement" is (1) an oral or written assertion or (2) nonverbal conduct of a person, if it is

intended as an assertion.

(b) Declarant. A "declarant" is a person who makes a statement.

(c) Hearsay. "Hearsay" is a statement, other than one made by the declarant while testifying at the trial or hearing, offered in evidence to prove the truth of the matter asserted.

Comparison and Commentary

The federal and Virginia rules employ the same hearsay definition. The Virginia definition differs only in its reliance on the pre-restyling federal language. Stevenson v. Com., 218 Va. 462, 465, 237 S.E.2d 779, 781 (Va. 1977) (citing hearsay definition in federal rules with approval). Notably, both definitions only capture words or actions that are intended as assertions, and include prior statements by testifying witnesses made out of court. See id.

The most conceptually difficult component of the federal-Virginia hearsay definition concerns assertive conduct and statements offered to prove something other than what was intended to be asserted. Such evidence is not hearsay under the federal rules. See Advisory Committee Note to Fed. R. Ev. 801(a) ("verbal conduct which is assertive but offered as a basis for inferring something other than the matter asserted" is "excluded from the definition of hearsay"). Thus, a letter informing the recipient of the difficult conditions in colonial Virginia would not be hearsay under the federal rules if offered to prove the sender's belief in the mental competence of the recipient. See Wright v. Tatham, 7 A. & E. 313, 112 Eng. Rep. 488 (Exch. Ch. 1837); Olin Guy Wellborn III, *The Definition of Hearsay in the Federal Rules of Evidence*, 61 Tex. L. Rev. 49, 93 (1982) (advocating a change to the federal definition to alter this result). The Virginia courts have not addressed this aspect of the hearsay definition. That said, there is Virginia case law finding out-of-court statements to be non-hearsay when introduced for a purpose other than to prove the truth of the matter intended to be asserted by the speaker. See Church v. Com., 230 Va. 208, 212, 335 S.E.2d 823, 825-26 (Va. 1985) ("The Commonwealth did not offer the child's statement to prove that sex is 'dirty, nasty and it hurt.' Rather, it was offered to show the child's attitude toward sex, an attitude likely to have been created by a traumatic experience."); Weller v. Com., 16 Va. App. 886, 895, 434 S.E.2d 330, 336 (Va. App. 1993) ("This evidence was not offered for the truth of its content-that Baker wanted to get her rings fixed by a jeweler in Silver Spring. Baker's statement the night before her death that she wanted to get her rings fixed was circumstantial evidence that she possessed the rings that night.") The principle actually articulated in the Virginia case law to support these decisions is that statements are not hearsay when admissible "as circumstantial evidence tending to establish the probability of a fact in issue." Church v. Com., 230 Va. 208, 212, 335 S.E.2d 823, 826 (Va. 1985). But the Virginia courts would do just as well to rely on the arguably more coherent rationale that out-of-court statements are not hearsay, as defined in Rule 2:801, when offered to prove something other than what the speaker was intending to assert. Of course, doing so narrows the hearsay definition, and perhaps uncomfortably so for some courts. For example, in Brown v. Com., 25 Va. App. 171, 179-80, 487 S.E.2d 248, 252 (Va. App. 1997), the Court of Appeals held that the question "'Does Peggy know I am here?'" was hearsay when offered to prove that the speaker knew Peggy because the declarant "was necessarily implying or asserting, 'I know Peggy personally.'" The Court of Appeals was correct that this is a necessary implication of the statement, but its hearsay status under the federal rules depends on whether the declarant intended to communicate this implication. The Court of Appeal's holding tracks not the Virginia-federal rule, but the Texas Rules of Evidence's distinct definitional supplement – courtesy of Professor Wellborn (cited above) – that "'[m]atter asserted' includes any matter explicitly asserted, and any matter implied by a statement, if the probative value of the statement as offered flows from declarant's belief as to the matter." Texas Rule of Evidence 801(c). Virginia's rule, of course, does not contain such a supplement.

Hearsay Statements of Testifying Witnesses

FED. R. EV. 801. ... EXCLUSIONS FROM HEARSAY

... (d) Statements That Are Not Hearsay. A statement that meets the following conditions is not hearsay:

(1) A Declarant-Witness's Prior Statement. The declarant testifies and is subject to cross-examination about a prior statement, and the statement:

(A) is inconsistent with the declarant's testimony and was given under penalty of perjury at a trial, hearing, or other proceeding or in a deposition;

(B) is consistent with the declarant's testimony and is offered:

(i) to rebut an express or implied charge that the declarant recently fabricated it or acted from a recent improper influence or motive in so testifying; or

(ii) to rehabilitate the declarant's credibility as a witness when attacked on another ground; or

(C) identifies a person as someone the declarant perceived earlier.

Va. R. Ev. 801 ... [effective July 2015]

...(d) Prior statements.

When a party or non-party witness testifies either live or by deposition, a prior statement (whether under oath or not) is hearsay if offered in evidence to prove the truth of the matters it asserts, but may be received in evidence for all purposes if the statement is admissible under any hearsay exception provided in Rules 2:803 or 2:804. In addition, if not excluded under another Rule of Evidence or a statute, a prior hearsay statement may also be admitted as follows:

(1) Prior inconsistent statements. A prior statement that is inconsistent with the hearing testimony of the witness is admissible for impeachment of the witness's credibility when offered in compliance with Rule 2:613.

(2) Prior consistent statements. A prior statement that is consistent with the hearing testimony of the witness is admissible for purposes of rehabilitating the witness's credibility, but only if

(A) the witness has been impeached using a prior inconsistent statement as provided in Rule 2:607, Rule 2:613 and/or subpart (d)(1) of this Rule 801, or

(B) (i) the witness has been impeached based on alleged improper influence, or a motive to falsify testimony, such as bias, interest, corruption or relationship to a party or a cause, or by an express or implied charge that the in-court testimony is a recent fabrication; and (ii) the proponent of the prior statement shows that it was made before any litigation motive arose for the witness to make a false statement.

VA. R. EV. 2:803(22) STATEMENT OF IDENTIFICATION BY WITNESS.

The declarant testifies at the trial or hearing and is subject to cross-examination concerning the statement, and the statement is one of identification of a person.

Comparison and Commentary

Federal Rule 801(d)(1)(A)-(C) exempts certain prior witness statements from the hearsay bar. Until July 2015, the Virginia rules included no analogue to Rule 801(d)(1)(A) or (B). And even after that date, in Virginia, all prior out-of-court statements (consistent or inconsistent with a witness' testimony) are not admissible for the truth of the matter asserted unless they fall within one of the explicit hearsay exceptions in the subsequent rules. See, e.g., Groggins v. Com., 34 Va. App. 19, 24, 537 S.E.2d 605, 607 (Va. App. 2000) ("A witness' prior inconsistent statement is admissible to impeach trial testimony but is not admissible to prove the truth of the matter asserted."); Mitchell v. Com., 25 Va. App. 81, 85, 486 S.E.2d 551, 553 (Va. App. 1997) (prior consistent statements are generally "inadmissible hearsay," but can be introduced to rehabilitate a testifying witness in certain circumstances; in such cases, "the statement is offered merely to show that it was made, rather than as proof of any matter asserted"). Rule 2:801(d)(1) (effective July 2015) states that prior inconsistent statements of testifying witnesses are admissible as impeachment, but this rule is superfluous; statements offered as impeachment are not offered for the truth of the matter asserted, and so are not objectionable as hearsay. Rule 2:801(d)(2) (effective July 2015) permits certain prior consistent statements to be utilized to rehabilitate a witness' credibility, again, a non-hearsay use that requires no special treatment in the hearsay rules. These provisions should be contrasted with their federal analogues which explicitly make qualifying statements admissible, not just as rehabilitation or impeachment, but for their truth.

Virginia possesses a close analogue to Federal Rule 801(d)(1)(C). Rule 2:803(22) parallels the unrevised federal 801(d)(1)(C), omitting only the text "after perceiving the person." There does not appear to be any significance to this omission. The Virginia case law permits not only testimony from the witness concerning her prior identification, but from a third party, such as a police officer, as well.

See Niblett v. Com., 217 Va. 76, 81, 225 S.E.2d 391, 394 (1976); cf. United States v. O'Malley, 796 F.2d 891, 899 (7th Cir. 1986). The Virginia codifiers admirably make this an exception to the hearsay rule, rather than defining qualifying statements as "not hearsay." That said, placement of the exception in Rule 803 is awkward because the rule begins with a statement that "[t]he following are not excluded by the hearsay rule, even though the declarant is available as a witness," while Rule 803(22), in fact, requires that the declarant testify.

Hearsay Statements of a Party

FED. R. EV. 801. ... EXCLUSIONS FROM HEARSAY

.... (d) Statements That Are Not Hearsay. A statement that meets the following conditions is not hearsay:

... (2) An Opposing Party's Statement. The statement is offered against an opposing party and:

> (A) was made by the party in an individual or representative capacity;

> (B) is one the party manifested that it adopted or believed to be true;

> (C) was made by a person whom the party authorized to make a statement on the subject;

> (D) was made by the party's agent or employee on a matter within the scope of that relationship and while it existed; or

> (E) was made by the party's coconspirator during and in furtherance of the conspiracy.

The statement must be considered but does not by itself establish the declarant's authority under (C); the existence or scope of the relationship under (D); or the existence of the conspiracy or participation in it under (E).

VA. R. EV. 2:803(0)

Admission by party-opponent. A statement offered against a party that is (A) the party's own statement, in either an individual or a representative capacity, or (B) a statement of which the party has manifested adoption or belief in its truth, or (C) a statement by a person authorized by the party to make a statement concerning the subject, or (D) a statement by the party's agent or employee, made during the term of the agency or employment, concerning a matter within the scope of such agency or employment, or (E) a statement by a co-conspirator of a party during the course and in furtherance of the conspiracy.

Comparison and Commentary

Virginia Rule 803(0) is the analogue to federal Rule 801(d)(2), excepting statements of a party opponent from the hearsay ban. A semantic distinction that arises from the distinct placements of the respective rules is that the Virginia rules view party opponent statements as exceptions to the hearsay prohibition, while the federal rules re-define such statements as "not hearsay." Nothing turns on this semantic distinction.

Another distinction is that Rule 803(0) does not include any language regarding what information can be considered in assessing whether a statement qualifies for admission under the agency, employee or co-conspirator exception. The federal rule states that the "hearsay" statement itself "must be considered" but cannot by itself establish the prerequisites for admission under Rule 801(d)(2)(C)-(E). The rule in Virginia is stricter, at least with respect to statements of co-conspirators:

"While other jurisdictions, most notably the federal courts, have relaxed the requirements for admissibility of a co-conspirator's hearsay statements when made in furtherance of the conspiracy, see Bourjaily v. U.S., 483 U.S. 171 (1987), the settled rule in Virginia remains that a prima facie case of conspiracy must be established by evidence independent of the hearsay declarations before those declarations may be admitted into evidence." Rabeiro v. Com., 10 Va. App. 61, 64, 389 S.E.2d 731, 732 (Va. App. 1990).

Thus, in Virginia, there must be "independent evidence of a conspiracy" from "which the existence of a conspiracy could reasonably be inferred." Floyd v. Com., 219 Va. 575, 582-83, 249 S.E.2d 171, 175 (Va. 1978); Anderson v. Com., 215 Va. 21, 24, 205 S.E.2d 393, 395 (Va. 1974) ("Such declarations are admissible even though a conspiracy is not charged where the evidence establishes a Prima facie case of conspiracy.") The requisite finding must be made "by a preponderance of the evidence." Jones v. Com., 11 Va. App. 75, 83, 396 S.E.2d 844, 848 (Va. App. 1990); cf. Lynch v. Com., 272 Va. 204, 208, 630 S.E.2d 482, 484 (Va. 2006) (noting that as a general matter, party claiming a hearsay exception applies carries the burden of persuasion and "[w]e have consistently held that the standard of proof to meet that burden is by a preponderance of the evidence").

Although the codified Virginia rule essentially tracks the federal rule's language with respect to employee statements, the case law in Virginia appears narrower, perhaps only allowing employee statements about a then-unfolding transaction or occurrence, rather than after-event statements. See Turner v. Norfolk S. Ry. Co., 205 Va. 691, 696, 139 S.E.2d 68, 72 (Va. 1964) (upholding exclusion of a railroad engineer's post-crash statement to police on the ground that the statement occurred outside "the immediate sphere of their agency"); Charles E. Friend and Kent Sinclair, The Law of Evidence in Virginia § 15-37 (7th ed. 2012) (noting that "[a]gents' statements made after the completion of an event are …, under Virginia practice, excluded" and adding as well that Virginia courts generally "exclud[e] admissions of minor employees").

FED. R. EV. 802. THE RULE AGAINST HEARSAY

Hearsay is not admissible unless any of the following provides otherwise:

- a federal statute;

- these rules; or

- other rules prescribed by the Supreme Court.

VA. R. EV. 2:802. HEARSAY RULE

Hearsay is not admissible except as provided by these Rules, other Rules of the Supreme Court of Virginia, or by Virginia statutes or case law.

Comparison and Commentary

Both the federal and Virginia rule 802 bars hearsay unless some other rule provides otherwise. The rules do not account for circumstances where constitutional provisions either require or forbid admission of hearsay. Importantly, the Virginia courts do not appear to have developed any state confrontation clause jurisprudence distinct from federal confrontation clause jurisprudence.

Rule 803 Editor's Introductory Note

Both the Virginia and federal rules contain a laundry list of hearsay exceptions that do not require the declarant to be unavailable. Due to their many subparts, these rules are compared by subpart below.

Fed. R. Ev. 803. Exceptions to the Rule Against Hearsay--Regardless of Whether the Declarant Is Available as a Witness

The following are not excluded by the rule against hearsay, regardless of whether the declarant is available as a witness:...

Va. R. Ev. 2:803. Hearsay Exceptions Applicable Regardless of Availability of the Declarant

The following are not excluded by the hearsay rule, even though the declarant is available as a witness:...

Va. R. Ev. 2:803 (0) [ed.- See Comparison and Commentary to Fed. R. Ev. 801.]

Fed. R. Ev. 803(1) Present Sense Impression. A statement describing or explaining an event or condition, made while or immediately after the declarant perceived it.

Va. R. Ev. 2:803(1) Present sense impression. A spontaneous statement describing or explaining an event or condition made contemporaneously with, or while, the declarant was perceiving the event or condition.

Comparison and Commentary

Both codes contain a hearsay exception for present sense impressions. The federal exception requires qualifying statements to be contemporaneous with a described event or uttered "immediately after." The Virginia rules only permit contemporaneous statements. Support can be found in the Virginia case law, however, for a short lag between event and description. Wilder v. Com., 55 Va. App. 579, 588, 687 S.E.2d 542, 546 (Va. App. 2010) (explaining that statements qualified as present sense impressions because they "were made contemporaneously *or near contemporaneously* with the acts they describe") (emphasis added).

Virginia's rule also requires the statement to be "spontaneous." This requirement, absent from the federal text, indicates that the statement must be an unplanned reaction to stimuli. Foley v. Com., 8 Va. App. 149, 164, 379 S.E.2d 915, 923 (Va. App. 1989) (affirming admission of comments during phone call as a present sense impression because, in part, the statement "was spontaneous, as it reflected Mrs. Foley's personal perceptions at that time and was not a narrative reflection of a past event"); Arnold v. Com., 4 Va. App. 275, 282, 356 S.E.2d 847, 851 (Va. App. 1987) (rejecting statement offered as a present sense impression where statement "was an act of deliberation" and thus "totally lacking spontaneity").

FED. R. EV. 803(2) EXCITED UTTERANCE. A statement relating to a startling event or condition, made while the declarant was under the stress of excitement that it caused.

VA. R. EV. 2:803 (2) EXCITED UTTERANCE. A spontaneous or impulsive statement prompted by a startling event or condition and made by a declarant with firsthand knowledge at a time and under circumstances negating deliberation.

Comparison and Commentary

Distinct from the federal variant, Virginia's excited utterance exception again requires that qualifying statements be "spontaneous" and "impulsive." The idea behind these requirements, drawn from the common law's amorphous "res gestae" exception, is that they further guarantee sincerity. Goins v. Com., 251 Va. 442, 460, 470 S.E.2d 114, 126 (Va. 1996) ("The statement must be prompted by a startling event and be made at such time and under such circumstances as to preclude the presumption that it was made as the result of deliberation."); Upton v. Com., 172 Va. 654, 657, 2 S.E.2d 337, 339 (Va. 1939) ("'In order for a declaration to be admissible as a part of the res gestae, it must be the spontaneous utterance of the mind, while under the influence of the transaction, the test being, it has been said, whether the declaration was the facts talking through the party or the party talking about the facts.'") The same concept resurfaces at the end of Virginia's excited utterance rule in its requirement that the statement arise "at a time and under circumstances negating deliberation." Writing these requirements into the rule itself, rather than anticipating their likely accompaniment of otherwise qualifying statements, suggests a stronger distrust of this type of hearsay than is found in the federal rules.

Virginia's requirement, set forth in the rule and case law, that "the declarant must have firsthand knowledge of the startling event," Goins v. Com., 251 Va. 442, 460, 470 S.E.2d 114, 126 (Va. 1996), mirrors the general requirement that a hearsay declarant, like any witness, possess personal knowledge of any information related to the factfinder. See Advisory Committee Note to Fed. R. Ev. 803 ("In a hearsay situation, the declarant is, of course, a witness, and neither this rule nor Rule 804 dispenses with the requirement of firsthand knowledge.") (citing Rule 602)).

FED. R. EV. 803(3) THEN-EXISTING MENTAL, EMOTIONAL, OR PHYSICAL CONDITION.

A statement of the declarant's then-existing state of mind (such as motive, intent, or plan) or emotional, sensory, or physical condition (such as mental feeling, pain, or bodily health), but not including a statement of memory or belief to prove the fact remembered or believed unless it relates to the validity or terms of the declarant's will.

VA. R. EV. 2:803(3) THEN EXISTING MENTAL, EMOTIONAL, OR PHYSICAL CONDITION. A statement of the declarant's then existing state of mind, emotion, sensation, or physical condition (such as intent, plan, motive, design, mental feeling, pain, and bodily health), but not including a statement of memory or belief to prove the fact remembered or believed unless it relates to the execution, revocation, identification, or terms of the declarant's will.

Comparison and Commentary

The Virginia and federal "state of mind" hearsay exception are essentially identical. There is some debate in the federal courts over whether a statement of intent that forecasts someone else's conduct is admissible as proof of that other person's conduct. See U.S. v. Pheaster, 544 F.2d 353, 376 (9th Cir. 1976) (setting forth the arguments on both sides of the debate). Virginia case law clearly allows such statements, following the seminal case of Mutual Life Insurance Co. v. Hillmon, 145 U.S. 285 (1892). See Hodges v. Com., 272 Va. 418, 443, 634 S.E.2d 680, 694 (2006).

FED. R. EV. 803(4) STATEMENT MADE FOR MEDICAL DIAGNOSIS OR TREATMENT. A statement that:

(A) is made for--and is reasonably pertinent to--medical diagnosis or treatment; and

(B) describes medical history; past or present symptoms or sensations; their inception; or their general cause.

VA. R. EV. 2:803(4) STATEMENTS FOR PURPOSES OF MEDICAL TREATMENT. Statements made for purposes of medical diagnosis or treatment and describing medical history, or past or present symptoms, pain, or sensations, or the inception or general character of the cause or external source thereof insofar as reasonably pertinent to diagnosis or treatment.

Comparison and Commentary

The Virginia and federal rules regarding statements for purposes of medical diagnosis or treatment are, on their face, identical. In fact, the Virginia rule uses the exact same language as the federal rule prior to restyling.

Importantly, however, while the Virginia Supreme Court's pronouncements on this exception are few, the extant Virginia case law seems significantly narrower than the codified rule. In the most recent case, the Court explained:

> "We have acknowledged that "a physician [may] testify to a patient's statements concerning his 'past pain, suffering and subjective symptoms' to show 'the basis of the physician's opinion as to the nature of the injuries or illness.'" Cartera v. Com., 219 Va. 516, 518, 248 S.E.2d 784, 785–86 (1978); accord Jenkins v. Com., 254 Va. 333, 339, 492 S.E.2d 131, 134 (1997)." Lawlor v. Com., 285 Va. 187, 243 (2013).

Lawlor and the two cases cited by *Lawlor* in the above excerpt are the three cases cited in the Virginia codification commentary to support Rule 2:803(4). But note that the *Lawlor* Court's description of the "exception" does not suggest that qualifying statements are admissible as substantive evidence, the normal effect of a hearsay exception. Instead, the Virginia Supreme Court explains that such statements to a physician are admissible to "show the basis of the physician's opinion" – a nonhearsay use that would not necessitate a hearsay exception. Further, one of the cited cases, *Jenkins*, contains the following passage, which is far from an endorsement of the exception:

> "The Commonwealth contends that we should apply the hearsay exception extended in some jurisdictions to statements made by a patient to a treating physician. As the Commonwealth recognized on brief, 'many of these out-of-state cases are

partially based on their state's adoption of rules equivalent to Federal Rule of Evidence 803(4).' Neither this Court nor the General Assembly has adopted any such rule." Jenkins v. Com., 254 Va. 333, 339, 492 S.E.2d 131, 134 (1997).

Thus, whether the Virginia courts have adopted a version of Federal Rule 803(4) is (at best) an open question. Whether the codification will succeed in its effort to answer that question remains to be seen.

Along these same lines, the federal rule applies beyond statements to a "treating physician," extending also to "statements to a physician consulted only for the purpose of enabling him to testify." Advisory Committee Note to Fed. R. Ev. 803(4). This extension appears as well in the Virginia rule ("or diagnosis"). Again, however, the Virginia Supreme Court's pronouncements cast doubt on the codification. In *Lawlor*, the Court endorsed a lower court's reasoning that statements made to a drug counselor should not fall under the exception because of doubts that "'a defendant who is incarcerated who talks to a drug counselor is going to be a hundred percent honest as one would who is seeking treatment from a physician.'" Lawlor v. Com., 285 Va. 187, 243, 738 S.E.2d 847, 879 (2013).

FED. R. EV. 803(5) RECORDED RECOLLECTION. A record that:

(A) is on a matter the witness once knew about but now cannot recall well enough to testify fully and accurately;

(B) was made or adopted by the witness when the matter was fresh in the witness's memory; and

(C) accurately reflects the witness's knowledge.

If admitted, the record may be read into evidence but may be received as an exhibit only if offered by an adverse party.

VA. R. EV. 2:803(5) RECORDED RECOLLECTION. Except as provided by statute, a memorandum or record concerning a matter about which a witness once had firsthand knowledge made or adopted by the witness at or near the time of the event and while the witness had a clear and accurate memory of it, if the witness lacks a present recollection of the event, and the witness vouches for the accuracy of the written memorandum. If admitted, the memorandum or record may be read into evidence but may not itself be received as an exhibit unless offered by an adverse party.

Comparison and Commentary

The Virginia and federal hearsay exceptions for "recorded recollections" are essentially the same. See Scott v. Greater Richmond Transit Co., 241 Va. 300, 304, 402 S.E.2d 214, 217 (1991) (relying on McCormick's treatise for requirements of the exception and citing federal rules' provision that the recording can be read to the jury but not received as an exhibit). Reliance on McCormick's treatise results in the Virginia rule replacing "when the matter was fresh in the witness's memory" with "at or near the time of the event," but the different terminology serves the same purpose. Similarly, the Virginia rule explicitly requires the witness to "vouch[] for the accuracy" of the recording, a requirement that is implicit in the federal variant, even though it is somewhat obscured in the restyled language. O'Malley v. U.S. Fid. & Guar. Co., 776 F.2d 494, 500 (5th Cir. 1985) ("The witness laying the foundation for evidence admitted under 803(5) must show the report to be accurate.") That said, the Virginia variant may require a more robust vouching than its federal counterpart. United States v. Porter, 986 F.2d 1014, 1017 (6th Cir. 1993) ("It is not a sine qua non of admissibility that the witness actually vouch for the accuracy of the written memorandum.")

FED. R. EV. 803(6) RECORDS OF A REGULARLY CONDUCTED ACTIVITY. A record of an act, event, condition, opinion, or diagnosis if:

(A) the record was made at or near the time by--or from information transmitted by--someone with knowledge;

(B) the record was kept in the course of a regularly conducted activity of a business, organization, occupation, or calling, whether or not for profit;

(C) making the record was a regular practice of that activity;

(D) all these conditions are shown by the testimony of the custodian or another qualified witness, or by a certification that complies with Rule 902(11) or (12) or with a statute permitting certification; and

(E) the opponent does not show that the source of information or the method or circumstances of preparation indicate a lack of trustworthiness.

VA. R. EV. 2:803(6) BUSINESS RECORDS. A memorandum, report, record, or data compilation, in any form, of acts, events, calculations or conditions, made at or near the time by, or from information transmitted by, a person with knowledge in the course of a regularly conducted business activity, and if it was the regular practice of that business activity to make and keep the memorandum, report, record, or data compilation, all as shown by the testimony of the custodian or other qualified witness, unless the source of information or the method or circumstances of preparation indicate lack of trustworthiness. The term "business" as used in this paragraph includes business, organization, institution, association, profession, occupation, and calling of every kind, whether or not conducted for profit.

VA. R. EV. 2:803(6) Records of a Regularly Conducted Activity. [ed. – new Rule 2:803(6) effective July 2015]

A record of acts, events, calculations, or conditions if:

(A) the record was made at or near the time of the acts, events, calculations, or conditions by – or from information transmitted by – someone with knowledge;

(B) the record was made and kept in the course of a regularly conducted activity of a business, organization, occupation, or calling, whether or not for profit;

(C) making and keeping the record was a regular practice of that activity;

(D) all these conditions are shown by the testimony of the custodian or another qualified witness, or by a certification that complies with Rule 2:902(6) or with a statute permitting certification; and

(E) neither the source of information or the method or circumstances of preparation indicate a lack of trustworthiness.

Comparison and Commentary

The Virginia and federal hearsay exception for business records contain almost identical language (and, as of July 2015, virtually identical form). Notably absent from the Virginia rule is any allowance for an "opinion" or "diagnosis" contained in a business record, matters explicitly covered by the federal exception. See Advisory Committee Note to Fed. R. Ev. 803(6) ("the rule specifically includes both diagnoses and opinions, in addition to acts, events, and conditions, as proper subjects of admissible entries"). As the Virginia Supreme Court explained in Neeley v. Johnson, the Virginia business records "exception has been generally restricted to facts or events within the personal knowledge and observation of the recorder to which he could testify if called as a witness." 215 Va. 565, 571, 211 S.E.2d 100, 106 (1975). Consequently, the Court "refuse[d] to extend the exception to include opinions and conclusions of physicians or others recorded in hospital records." Id. The Virginia Supreme Court more recently loosened the personal knowledge requirement, holding that: "In certain cases, where verification of the recorded facts is not possible through the personal knowledge of the record keeper, practical necessity nevertheless requires admission of recorded evidence which has a circumstantial guarantee of trustworthiness; this guarantee is provided where evidence shows the regularity of the preparation of the records and reliance on them by their preparers or those for whom they are prepared." Frye v. Com., 231 Va. 370, 387, 345 S.E.2d 267, 279-80 (1986). Virginia's rule explicitly covers "calculations," something that the federal rule likely captures implicitly.

As under the federal rule, statements captured in business records that were made by "outsiders" to the business, are not covered by Virginia's business records exception. Ford Motor Co. v. Phelps, 239 Va. 272, 276, 389 S.E.2d 454, 457 (1990) ("[T]he consumers, who either made the complaints themselves (or through counsel) or who furnished the information to Ford employees from which the records of the complaints were made, were not acting in the regular course of business."); United States v. Vigneau, 187 F.3d 70, 76 (1st Cir. 1999) (federal business records exception "excludes this 'outsider' information, where offered for its truth, unless some other hearsay exception applies to the outsider's own statement").

FED. R. EV. 803(7) ABSENCE OF A RECORD OF A REGULARLY CONDUCTED ACTIVITY. Evidence that a matter is not included in a record described in paragraph (6) if:

(A) the evidence is admitted to prove that the matter did not occur or exist;

(B) a record was regularly kept for a matter of that kind; and

(C) the opponent does not show that the possible source of the information or other circumstances indicate a lack of trustworthiness.

Comparison and Commentary

Unlike the federal rules, the Virginia rules do not include a hearsay exception for the absence of an entry in a business record. This distinction does not signal any real difference between the two jurisdictions. As the Advisory Committee Note to Rule 803(7) acknowledges, the absence of an entry in a record is "probably not hearsay as defined in Rule 801" and so no exception is technically required. Further, if the absence of an entry is sought to be established, the proponent of the evidence could presumably introduce the record itself to establish the absence of anything from the record.

FED. R. EV. 803(8) PUBLIC RECORDS. A record or statement of a public office if:

(A) it sets out:

> **(i)** the office's activities;

> **(ii)** a matter observed while under a legal duty to report, but not including, in a criminal case, a matter observed by law-enforcement personnel; or

> **(iii)** in a civil case or against the government in a criminal case, factual findings from a legally authorized investigation; and

(B) the opponent does not show that the source of information or other circumstances indicate a lack of trustworthiness.

VA. R. EV. 2:803(8) PUBLIC RECORDS AND REPORTS. In
addition to categories of government records made admissible
by statute, records, reports, statements, or data compilations,
in any form, prepared by public offices or agencies, setting forth
(A) the activities of the office or agency, or (B) matters observed
within the scope of the office or agency's duties, as to which the
source of the recorded information could testify if called as a
witness; generally excluding, however, in criminal cases
matters observed by police officers and other law enforcement
personnel when offered against a criminal defendant.

Comparison and Commentary

The Virginia hearsay exception for public records differs somewhat
from the federal exception. With respect to the second, and most
widely used, category of public records, the two rules subtly diverge
in a manner that likely has little substantive effect. The federal
exception covers "matters observed while under a legal duty to
report." The Virginia exception applies to "matters observed within
the scope of the office's ... duty." While the Virginia exception
appears broader, the federal rule is generally interpreted along the
lines of the Virginia text.

The Virginia rule also diverges from the federal text in stating that the
"source" of the recorded information must (hypothetically) be able to
"testify to the information if called as a witness" – a requirement not
explicitly contained in the federal rule. The Virginia restriction means
that a public document is only admissible to the extent "the
document relates facts or events within the personal knowledge and
observation of the recording official to which he could testify should
he be called as a witness." Williams v. Com., 213 Va. 45, 46, 189
S.E.2d 378, 379 (1972). This caveat is generally required by the
federal rules for all hearsay declarants, and so it is understandable that
it would not be written into the federal exception. See Advisory
Committee Note to Fed. R. Ev. 803 ("In a hearsay situation, the

declarant is, of course, a witness, and neither this rule nor Rule 804 dispenses with the requirement of first-hand knowledge.") That said, Virginia's requirement of personal knowledge, in concert with the absence of a direct analogue to Rule 803(8)(A)(iii), signals that public records relating hearsay statements of someone other than the recording official will not be admissible under the Virginia exception. Contrast Beech Aircraft Corp. v. Rainey, 488 U.S. 153, 154 (1988) (interpreting federal exception to cover the full content of reports that include "factual findings from a legally authorized investigation"); see also Va. Code § 46.2-379 (barring "crash reports made by investigating officers" from admission into evidence).

The Virginia exception also differs from the federal analogue in that it does not contain the catch-all authorization for exclusion where "the source of information or other circumstances indicate a lack of trustworthiness."

Other Pertinent Virginia Provisions

With respect to judicial records, Virginia Code § 8.01-389 states:

(A) "The records of any judicial proceeding and any other official records of any court of this Commonwealth shall be received as prima facie evidence provided that such records are certified by the clerk of the court where preserved to be a true record...."

(A1) "The records of any judicial proceeding and any other official record of any court of another state or country, or of the United States, shall be received as prima facie evidence provided that such records are certified by the clerk of the court where preserved to be a true record."

See also discussion of Rule 2:203 ("Judicial Notice of Official Publications"), above, and Va. Code § 8.01-388 (same); Va. Code § 8.01-390.1 ("In a proceeding where a minor's school records are material and otherwise admissible, copies of such school records shall be received as evidence in any matter, provided that such copies are authenticated to be true and accurate copies by the custodian thereof, or by the person to whom the custodian reports if they are different."); Va. Code sec. 8.01-387 (requiring courts to take judicial notice "of the signature of any of the judges, or of the Governor of this Commonwealth, to any judicial or official document").

FED. R. EV. 803(9) PUBLIC RECORDS OF VITAL STATISTICS. A record of a birth, death, or marriage, if reported to a public office in accordance with a legal duty.

VA. R. EV. 2: 803(9) RECORDS OF VITAL STATISTICS. Records or data compilations, in any form, of births, fetal deaths, deaths, or marriages, if the report was made to a public office pursuant to requirements of law.

Comparison and Commentary

The Virginia and federal rules contain an identical hearsay exception for records of vital statistics. See also Rule 2:203 ("Judicial Notice of Official Publications") and Va. Code § 8.01-388 (same).

FED. R. EV. 803(10) ABSENCE OF A PUBLIC RECORD.
Testimony--or a certification under Rule 902--that a diligent search failed to disclose a public record or statement if:

(A) the testimony or certification is admitted to prove that

(i) the record or statement does not exist; or

(ii) a matter did not occur or exist, if a public office regularly kept a record or statement for a matter of that kind; and

(B) in a criminal case, a prosecutor who intends to offer a certification provides written notice of that intent at least 14 days before trial, and the defendant does not object in writing within 7 days of receiving the notice--unless the court sets a different time for the notice or the objection.

VA. R. EV. 2:803(10) ABSENCE OF ENTRIES IN PUBLIC RECORDS AND REPORTS.

(a) Civil Cases. An affidavit signed by an officer, or the deputy thereof, deemed to have custody of records of this Commonwealth, of another state, of the United States, of another country, or of any political subdivision or agency of the same, other than those located in a clerk's office of a court, stating that after a diligent search, no record or entry of such record is found to exist among the records in such office is admissible as evidence that the office has no such record or entry.

(b) Criminal Cases. In any criminal hearing or trial, an affidavit signed by a government official who is competent to testify, deemed to have custody of an official record, or signed by such official's designee, stating that after a diligent search, no record or entry of such record is found to exist among the records in such official's custody, is admissible as evidence that the office has no such record or entry, provided that if the hearing or trial is a proceeding other than a preliminary hearing the procedures set forth in subsection G of § 18.2-472.1 for admission of an affidavit have been satisfied, *mutatis mutandis*, and the accused has not objected to the admission of the affidavit pursuant to the procedures set forth in subsection H of § 18.2-472.1, *mutatis mutandis*. Nothing in this subsection (b) shall be construed to affect the admissibility of affidavits in civil cases under subsection (a) of this Rule.

Comparison and Commentary

The Virginia and federal rules provide an exception to the hearsay prohibition for an affidavit or certification by a public official attesting that a search of public records revealed that there is no such record in the public files. Both rules provide the defendant in a criminal case an opportunity to object to application of the exception. A defendant's timely objection is dispositive under both rules, rendering the respective hearsay exception inapplicable. Va. Code § 18.2-472.1(H) ("If timely objection is made, the affidavit shall not be admissible into evidence unless (i) the objection is waived by the accused or his counsel in writing or before the court, or (ii) the parties stipulate before the court to the admissibility of the affidavit.") See also Va. Code § 8.01-390 (C) ("An affidavit signed by an officer deemed to have custody of such an official record, or by his deputy, stating that after a diligent search, no record or entry of such record is found to exist among the records in his office is admissible as evidence that his office has no such record or entry.")

Virginia's rule, by its terms, does not apply to records "located in a clerk's office of a court." This curious carve out does not preclude admission of similar evidence regarding an absence of an entry or document in judicial records. Instead, this is undoubtedly a drafting artifact. Rule 2:803(10), including the quoted carve out comes directly from Va. Code § 8.01-390 ("Nonjudicial records as evidence"), which follows sequentially Va. Code § 8.01-389 ("Judicial records as evidence"). The carve out clarifies that, as § 8.01-390's title suggests, judicial records are not covered by the section. Instead, they are treated separately in § 8.01-389, which liberally admits evidence of such records.

FED. R. EV. 803(11) RECORDS OF RELIGIOUS ORGANIZATIONS CONCERNING PERSONAL OR FAMILY HISTORY. A statement of birth, legitimacy, ancestry, marriage, divorce, death, relationship by blood or marriage, or similar facts of personal or family history, contained in a regularly kept record of a religious organization.

VA. R. EV. 2:803 (11) RECORDS OF RELIGIOUS ORGANIZATIONS.

Statements of births, marriages, divorces, deaths, legitimacy, ancestry, relationship by blood or marriage, or other similar facts of personal or family history, contained in a regularly kept record of a religious organization.

Comparison and Commentary

The Virginia and federal hearsay exceptions for records of religious organizations are the same.

FED. R. EV. 803(12) CERTIFICATES OF MARRIAGE, BAPTISM, AND SIMILAR CEREMONIES.

A statement of fact contained in a certificate:

(A) made by a person who is authorized by a religious organization or by law to perform the act certified;

(B) attesting that the person performed a marriage or similar ceremony or administered a sacrament; and

(C) purporting to have been issued at the time of the act or within a reasonable time after it.

VA. R. EV. 2:803(12) MARRIAGE, BAPTISMAL, AND SIMILAR CERTIFICATES.

Statements of fact contained in a certificate that the maker performed a marriage or other ceremony or administered a sacrament, made by a clergyman, public official, or other person authorized by the rules or practices of a religious organization or by law to perform the act certified, and purporting to have been issued at the time of the act or within a reasonable time thereafter.

Comparison and Commentary

The Virginia and federal hearsay exceptions for marriage, baptismal and similar certificates are the same.

FED. R. EV. 803(13) FAMILY RECORDS. A statement of fact about personal or family history contained in a family record, such as a Bible, genealogy, chart, engraving on a ring, inscription on a portrait, or engraving on an urn or burial marker.

VA. R. EV. 2:803(13) FAMILY RECORDS. Statements of fact concerning personal or family history contained in family bibles, genealogies, charts, engravings on rings, inscriptions on family portraits, engravings on urns, crypts, or tombstones, or the like.

Comparison and Commentary

The Virginia and federal hearsay exceptions for family records are the same.

FED. R. EV. 803(14) RECORDS OF DOCUMENTS THAT AFFECT AN INTEREST IN PROPERTY. The record of a document that purports to establish or affect an interest in property if:

(A) the record is admitted to prove the content of the original recorded document, along with its signing and its delivery by each person who purports to have signed it;

(B) the record is kept in a public office; and

(C) a statute authorizes recording documents of that kind in that office.

VA. R. EV. 2:803(14) RECORDS OF DOCUMENTS AFFECTING AN INTEREST IN PROPERTY. The record of a document purporting to establish or affect an interest in property, as proof of the content of the original recorded document and its execution, and delivery by each person by whom it purports to have been executed, if the record is a record of a public office and an applicable statute authorizes the recording of documents of that kind in that office.

Comparison and Commentary

The Virginia and federal hearsay exceptions for records affecting an interest in property are the same.

FED. R. EV. 803(15) STATEMENTS IN DOCUMENTS THAT AFFECT AN INTEREST IN PROPERTY. A statement contained in a document that purports to establish or affect an interest in property if the matter stated was relevant to the document's purpose--unless later dealings with the property are inconsistent with the truth of the statement or the purport of the document.

VA. R. EV. 2:803(15) STATEMENTS IN DOCUMENTS AFFECTING AN INTEREST IN PROPERTY. A statement contained in a document purporting to establish or affect an interest in property if the matter stated was relevant to the purpose of the document, unless dealings with the property since the document was made have been inconsistent with the truth of the statement or the purport of the document.

Comparison and Commentary

The Virginia and federal hearsay exceptions for statements in a document affecting an interest in property are the same. See also Va. Code § 8.01-389(C) ("recitals of any fact in a deed or deed of trust of record conveying any interest in real property shall be prima facie evidence of that fact").

FED. R. EV. 803(16) STATEMENTS IN ANCIENT DOCUMENTS. A statement in a document that is at least 20 years old and whose authenticity is established.

VA. R. EV. 2:803(16) STATEMENTS IN ANCIENT DOCUMENTS. Statements generally acted upon as true by persons having an

interest in the matter, and contained in a document in existence 30 years or more, the authenticity of which is established.

Comparison and Commentary

The Virginia "ancient documents" hearsay exception requires a longer passage of time (30 years) than the federal rule (20 years). The Virginia rule also purports (as did the federal rule) to resolve ambiguity in the case law as to whether the rule applied only to authentication, as opposed to admitting hearsay within the ancient document. The Virginia codifiers boldly state that their identification of this rule "as a hearsay exception" resolves "any ambiguity over the possible limitation of ancient documents doctrine to foundational matters." See Codification Commentary to Rule 2:803(16); Friend & Sinclair § 15-28 at 1064-65; but see Rule 2:102 (stating that the rules "are adopted to implement established principles under the common law and not to change any established case law rendered prior to the adoption of the Rules").

The Virginia rule limits the doctrine to statements "generally acted upon as true by persons having an interest in the matter." This restriction appears to be derived from California's evidence code. See Cal. Ev. Code § 1331 ("Evidence of a statement is not made inadmissible by the hearsay rule if the statement is contained in a writing more than 30 years old and the statement has been since generally acted upon as true by persons having an interest in the matter.") There is no case law in Virginia and little elsewhere explaining what type of a showing is required to satisfy this requirement.

FED. R. EV. 803(17) MARKET REPORTS AND SIMILAR COMMERCIAL PUBLICATIONS. Market quotations, lists, directories, or other compilations that are generally relied on by the public or by persons in particular occupations.

VA. R. EV. 2:803(17) MARKET QUOTATIONS. Whenever the prevailing price or value of any goods regularly bought and sold in any established commodity market is in issue, reports in official publications or trade journals or in newspapers or periodicals of general circulation published as the reports of such market shall be admissible in evidence. The circumstances of the preparation of such a report may be shown.

Comparison and Commentary

The Virginia market quotations hearsay exception is narrower than the federal analogue. The Virginia exception only applies to the "price or value" of goods, while the federal exception applies not only to price quotes, but also to "lists, directories and other compilations." The Virginia limitation traces to the statute from which the exception is derived, Va. Code § 8.2-724.

FED. R. EV. 803(18) STATEMENTS IN LEARNED TREATISES, PERIODICALS, OR PAMPHLETS. A statement contained in a treatise, periodical, or pamphlet if:

(A) the statement is called to the attention of an expert witness on cross-examination or relied on by the expert on direct examination; and

(B) the publication is established as a reliable authority by the expert's admission or testimony, by another expert's testimony, or by judicial notice.

If admitted, the statement may be read into evidence but not received as an exhibit.

VA. R. EV. 2:706. USE OF LEARNED TREATISES WITH EXPERTS (Rule 2:706(a) derived from Code § 8.01-401.1)

(a) Civil cases. To the extent called to the attention of an expert witness upon cross-examination or relied upon by the expert witness in direct examination, statements contained in published treatises, periodicals or pamphlets on a subject of history, medicine or other science or art, established as a reliable authority by testimony or by stipulation shall not be excluded as hearsay. If admitted, the statements may be read into evidence but may not be received as exhibits. If the statements are to be introduced through an expert witness upon direct examination, copies of the specific statements shall be designated as literature to be introduced during direct examination and provided to opposing parties 30 days prior to trial unless otherwise ordered by the court. If a statement has been designated by a party in accordance with and satisfies the requirements of this rule, the expert witness called by that party need not have relied on the statement at the time of forming his opinion in order to read the statement into evidence during direct examination at trial.

(b) Criminal cases. Where an expert witness acknowledges on cross-examination that a published work is a standard authority in the field, an opposing party may ask whether the witness agrees or disagrees with statements in the work acknowledged. Such proof shall be received solely for impeachment purposes with respect to the expert's credibility.

Comparison and Commentary

Virginia's treatment of learned treatises is not in Rule 2:803, but can be found instead in the rules addressing expert testimony, specifically, Rule 2:706. The Virginia and federal provisions are largely the same with respect to civil cases, although Virginia includes a notice provision that is absent from the federal exception.

Virginia's rule for criminal cases, however, is not a hearsay exception at all. Instead, and contrary to the federal rule, it merely permits statements from acknowledged learned treatises to be utilized for the non-hearsay purpose of "impeachment" of expert witnesses.

FED. R. EV. 803(19) REPUTATION CONCERNING PERSONAL OR FAMILY HISTORY. A reputation among a person's family by blood, adoption, or marriage--or among a person's associates or in the community--concerning the person's birth, adoption, legitimacy, ancestry, marriage, divorce, death, relationship by blood, adoption, or marriage, or similar facts of personal or family history.

Comparison and Commentary

While providing a hearsay exception for judgments regarding family history, 2:803(21), Virginia's evidence rules do not contain an analogue to Federal Rule 803(19). Instead, Virginia's rule 803(19) is analogous to Federal Rule 803(20). As a result, the numbering of the balance of Rule 803 becomes misaligned (see below). As noted below, the text of Virginia's rule 2:803(21) implies that a rule like Federal Rule 803(19) should be included in the Virginia Code.

FED. R. EV. 803(20) REPUTATION CONCERNING BOUNDARIES OR GENERAL HISTORY. A reputation in a community--arising before the controversy--concerning boundaries of land in the community or customs that affect the land, or concerning general historical events important to that community, state, or nation.

VA. R. EV. 2:803(19) REPUTATION CONCERNING BOUNDARIES. Reputation in a community, arising before the controversy, as to boundaries of lands in the community, where the reputation refers to monuments or other delineations on the ground and some evidence of title exists.

Comparison and Commentary

The Virginia and federal rules contain a hearsay exception for community understandings of land boundaries. The federal rule also extends to historical events, while the Virginia rule does not.

FED. R. EV. 803 (21) REPUTATION CONCERNING CHARACTER.
A reputation among a person's associates or in the community concerning the person's character.

VA. R. EV. 2:803(20) REPUTATION AS TO A CHARACTER TRAIT.
Reputation of a person's character trait among his or her associates or in the community.

Comparison and Commentary

The federal and Virginia rules have an identical hearsay exception for character reputation testimony. Virginia's is labeled 2:803(20), while the federal analogue is Rule 803(21).

FED. R. EV. 803(22) JUDGMENT OF A PREVIOUS CONVICTION.
Evidence of a final judgment of conviction if:

(A) the judgment was entered after a trial or guilty plea, but not a nolo contendere plea;

(B) the conviction was for a crime punishable by death or by imprisonment for more than a year;

(C) the evidence is admitted to prove any fact essential to the judgment; and

(D) when offered by the prosecutor in a criminal case for a purpose other than impeachment, the judgment was against the defendant.

The pendency of an appeal may be shown but does not affect admissibility.

Comparison and Commentary

Unlike the federal rules, the Virginia evidence code does not contain a hearsay exception allowing a judgment of conviction to be admitted over a hearsay objection. Virginia Rule 2:609 does note that a conviction can be "proved by extrinsic evidence" in certain circumstances, but there is no matching provision for proof by hearsay in Rule 2:803. Virginia case law recognizes, however, that convictions can be proven by hearsay in the form of certified records. Essex v. Com., 18 Va. App. 168, 171, 442 S.E.2d 707, 709 (1994) ("The most efficient way to prove the prior felony conviction is to offer in evidence an authenticated copy of the prior order of conviction.")

FED. R. EV. 803(23) JUDGMENTS INVOLVING PERSONAL, FAMILY, OR GENERAL HISTORY, OR A BOUNDARY. A judgment that is admitted to prove a matter of personal, family, or general history, or boundaries, if the matter:

(A) was essential to the judgment; and

(B) could be proved by evidence of reputation.

VA. R. EV. 2:803(21) JUDGMENT AS TO PERSONAL, FAMILY, OR GENERAL HISTORY, OR BOUNDARIES. Judgments as proof of matters of personal, family or general history, or boundaries, essential to the judgment, if the same would be provable by evidence of reputation.

Comparison and Commentary

The federal and Virginia rules contain a hearsay exception for judgments related to family or general history or boundaries, although the rule numbers do not align. Both rules require the subject to be "provable by evidence of reputation." Strangely, however, the Virginia rules (unlike the federal rules – see Rule 803(19)) do not provide a hearsay exception for reputation "evidence of personal, family or general history."

VA. R. Ev. 2:803(22) STATEMENT OF IDENTIFICATION BY WITNESS. [ed.--See discussion under Fed. R. Ev. 801]

VA. R. Ev. 2:803(23) RECENT COMPLAINT OF SEXUAL ASSAULT. In any prosecution for criminal sexual assault under Article 7 (§ 18.2-61 et seq.) of Chapter 4 of Title 18.2, a violation of §§ 18.2-361, 18.2-366, 18.2-370 or § 18.2-370.1 [ed.-- fornication, incest, child molestation, etc.], the fact that the person injured made complaint of the offense recently after commission of the offense is admissible, not as independent evidence of the offense, but for the purpose of corroborating the testimony of the complaining witness.

Comparison and Commentary

The federal rules do not contain an analogue to Virginia's "recent complaint of sexual assault" exception. The Virginia rule is copied verbatim from Va. Code §19.2-268.2. The rule's placement as a hearsay exception in Rule 2:803 is questionable, since statements admitted under the rule do not come in as "evidence of the offense," but only for the "purpose of corroborating the testimony of the complaining witness." Nonetheless, Virginia's rule resonates with the recent amendment to Fed. R. Ev. 801(d)(1)(B)(ii), which provides a hearsay exception for prior witness statements offered "to rehabilitate the declarant's credibility as a witness when attacked on another ground."

VA. R. Ev. 2:803(24) PRICE OF GOODS. In shoplifting cases, price tags regularly affixed to items of personalty offered for sale, or testimony concerning the amounts shown on such tags.

Comparison and Commentary

There is no federal analogue to Rule 803(24). The rule is derived from Robinson v. Com., 258 Va. 3, 10 (1999). For further discussion, see Comparison and Commentary to Rule 807.

RULE 804 EDITOR'S INTRODUCTORY NOTE

Both the Virginia and federal rules contain a number of hearsay exceptions that require the declarant to be unavailable. Due to their many subparts, these rules are discussed by subpart below.

FED. R. EV. 804. EXCEPTIONS TO THE RULE AGAINST HEARSAY--WHEN THE DECLARANT IS UNAVAILABLE AS A WITNESS

(a) Criteria for Being Unavailable. A declarant is considered to be unavailable as a witness if the declarant:

> **(1)** is exempted from testifying about the subject matter of the declarant's statement because the court rules that a privilege applies;
>
> **(2)** refuses to testify about the subject matter despite a court order to do so;
>
> **(3)** testifies to not remembering the subject matter;
>
> **(4)** cannot be present or testify at the trial or hearing because of death or a then-existing infirmity, physical illness, or mental illness; or
>
> **(5)** is absent from the trial or hearing and the statement's proponent has not been able, by process or other reasonable means, to procure:
>
> > **(A)** the declarant's attendance, in the case of a hearsay exception under Rule 804(b)(1) or (6); or
> >
> > **(B)** the declarant's attendance or testimony, in the case of a hearsay exception under Rule 804(b)(2), (3), or (4).

But this subdivision (a) does not apply if the statement's

proponent procured or wrongfully caused the declarant's unavailability as a witness in order to prevent the declarant from attending or testifying.

VA. R. EV. 2:804. HEARSAY EXCEPTIONS APPLICABLE WHERE THE DECLARANT IS UNAVAILABLE (Rule 2:804(B)(5) derived from Code § 8.01-397)

(a) Applicability. The hearsay exceptions set forth in subpart (b) hereof are applicable where the declarant is dead or otherwise unavailable as a witness.

Comparison and Commentary

As is apparent, the federal and Virginia hearsay exceptions follow a similar pattern. For Rule 803 exceptions, the declarant need not be unavailable; for Rule 804 exceptions, the declarant must be unavailable. Federal Rule 804(a) sets forth specific criteria that constitute "unavailability"; Virginia, by contrast, lists one type of unavailability (death), but leaves all other species of unavailability unspecified. Nevertheless, the Virginia case law mirrors the federal forms of unavailability. A commonly cited list, includes:

> "(1) The declarant is dead. (2) The declarant is too ill to testify. (3) The declarant is insane. (4) The declarant is absent from the state and the party is unable to obtain the declarant's deposition. (5) The party has been unable by diligent inquiry to locate the declarant. (6) The declarant cannot be compelled to testify. (7) The opposite party has caused the declarant's absence."

Doan v. Com., 15 Va. App. 87, 100-01, 422 S.E.2d 398, 406 (1992) (quoting Charles E. Friend, The Law of Evidence in Virginia § 231 (3d ed. 1988)).

As in the federal rule, lack of memory can constitute unavailability, however, the Virginia Supreme Court has stressed that "the bona fides of a claim of loss of memory must be tested." Sapp v. Com., 263 Va. 415, 427, 559 S.E.2d 645, 651 (2002).

In both the federal and Virginia system, a defendant cannot create his own unavailability for purposes of the rule by invoking his Fifth Amendment privilege. See Bailey v. Com., 62 Va. App. 499, 509, 749 S.E.2d 544, 549 (2013) (announcing principle and recognizing that "[n]umerous federal and state courts, applying similar legal principles, have reached this same conclusion"). Although not indicated in the rule, Virginia case law parallels the federal rule provision that bars a proponent of hearsay who caused the declarant's unavailability from taking advantage of Rule 804. *Doan*, at 101.

The federal rule suggests that for dying declarations, statements against interest, and statements of family history, unavailability requires a showing that the hearsay proponent could not procure the declarant's "attendance" or "testimony," i.e., a deposition of the declarant. See Congressional Conference Report to Fed. R. Ev. 804(a) ("such as by deposition or interrogatories"). The Virginia rule does not require the proponent to have endeavored to depose or submit interrogatories to a party to establish their later unavailability – a sensible choice in the criminal context in which these exceptions are generally invoked.

FED. R. EV. 804(B) THE EXCEPTIONS. The following are not excluded by the rule against hearsay if the declarant is unavailable as a witness:

(1) FORMER TESTIMONY. Testimony that:

> **(A)** was given as a witness at a trial, hearing, or lawful deposition, whether given during the current proceeding or a different one; and

> **(B)** is now offered against a party who had--or, in a

civil case, whose predecessor in interest had--an opportunity and similar motive to develop it by direct, cross-, or redirect examination.

VA. R. EV. 2:804. HEARSAY EXCEPTIONS APPLICABLE WHERE THE DECLARANT IS UNAVAILABLE

(B) HEARSAY EXCEPTIONS. The following are not excluded by the hearsay rule:

(1) FORMER TESTIMONY. Testimony given under oath or otherwise subject to penalties for perjury at a prior hearing, or in a deposition, if it is offered in reasonably accurate form and, if given in a different proceeding, the party against whom the evidence is now offered, or in a civil case a privy, was a party in that proceeding who examined the witness by direct examination or had the opportunity to cross-examine the witness, and the issue on which the testimony is offered is substantially the same in the two cases.

Comparison and Commentary

The Virginia and federal rules contain a hearsay exception for former testimony by an unavailable witness. The rules both require the qualifying statements to have been made in a formal "proceeding," such as a pretrial hearing or deposition, and require that the party against whom the statement is offered possessed an opportunity and similar incentive to develop that testimony in the prior proceeding.

The Virginia rule can be read to only require a similar motive to develop the prior testimony when the testimony was "given in a *different* proceeding." Rule 2:804(1) (emphasis added); see, e.g., Longshore v. Com., 260 Va. 3, 4, 530 S.E.2d 146, 146 (2000) (emphasizing requirement that the adverse party have been "afforded the opportunity of cross-examination when the witness testified at the preliminary hearing," but not discussing whether issues and motive for such examination were the same). This would mean that prior testimony from the same proceeding (e.g., testimony by a witness in a preliminary hearing or suppression hearing who becomes unavailable at the trial in same case) would be admissible in Virginia courts regardless of differences in the issues and motive to cross-examine. That is not the case in the federal system where motive remains a critical inquiry whether the prior testimony occurred in the same or a different proceeding. See, e.g., United States v. Duenas, 691 F.3d 1070, 1089 (9th Cir. 2012). This arguable distinction in the Virginia rule would also make it easier for Virginia defense attorneys to offer exculpatory grand jury testimony from unavailable witnesses, something that can be difficult in federal prosecutions. See United States v. Dinapoli, 8 F.3d 909 (2d Cir. 1993) (concluding that grand jury testimony offered was not admissible because prosecution's motive to develop the testimony was not sufficiently similar).

A separate Virginia statute allows written authentication of a transcript of a prior proceeding. See Va. Code § 8.01-420.3 ("Whenever a party seeks to introduce the transcript or record of the testimony of a witness at an earlier trial, hearing or deposition, it shall not be necessary for the reporter to be present to prove the transcript or record, provided the reporter duly certifies, in writing, the accuracy of the transcript or record.")

FED. R. EV. 804(B)(2) STATEMENT UNDER THE BELIEF OF IMMINENT DEATH.
In a prosecution for homicide or in a civil case, a statement that the declarant, while believing the declarant's death to be imminent, made about its cause or circumstances.

VA. R. EV. 2:804(B)(2) STATEMENT UNDER BELIEF OF IMPENDING DEATH.
In a prosecution for homicide, a statement made by a declarant who believed when the statement was

made that death was imminent and who had given up all hope of survival, concerning the cause or circumstances of declarant's impending death.

Comparison and Commentary

The Virginia and federal rules contain a hearsay exception for dying declarations. The federal rule applies in civil cases and homicide prosecutions. Virginia's rule applies exclusively in homicide prosecutions. The rules are otherwise parallel, although Virginia morbidly echoes the famous case of Shepard v. United States, 290 U.S. 96, 99 (1933) ("settled hopeless expectation") in its requirement that the declarant have "given up all hope of survival."

FED. R. EV. 804(B)(3) STATEMENT AGAINST INTEREST. A statement that:

(A) a reasonable person in the declarant's position would have made only if the person believed it to be true because, when made, it was so contrary to the declarant's proprietary or pecuniary interest or had so great a tendency to invalidate the declarant's claim against someone else or to expose the declarant to civil or criminal liability; and

(B) is supported by corroborating circumstances that clearly indicate its trustworthiness, if it is offered in a criminal case as one that tends to expose the declarant to criminal liability.

VA. R. EV. 2:804(B)(3) STATEMENT AGAINST INTEREST. (A) A statement which the declarant knew at the time of its making to be contrary to the declarant's pecuniary or proprietary interest, or to tend to subject the declarant to civil liability. (B) A statement which the declarant knew at the time of its making would tend to subject the declarant to criminal liability, if the statement is shown to be reliable.

Comparison and Commentary

The Virginia and federal exceptions for "statements against interest" are conceptually similar but distinct in emphasis. Both allow statements against financial or penal interests. Both require that statements offered as against penal interest be supported by indicia of reliability. The federal rule appears to require a stronger measure of against-interest for qualifying statements. It requires that a qualifying statement be "so contrary to the declarant's" interest that "a reasonable person in the declarant's position would have made" the statement "only if the person believed it to be true." The Virginia rule, by contrast requires only that the declarant be aware that the statement was contrary to his (monetary or criminal) interest. Of course not every statement implicating a defendant in a crime will qualify as "against interest" even under this more lenient standard. See Schmitt v. Com., 262 Va. 127, 144, 547 S.E.2d 186, 198 (2001).

In both Virginia and the federal system, each individual assertion contained within a longer "statement" must be evaluated independently for its against-interest quality. See Schmitt v. Com., 262 Va. 127, 144, 547 S.E.2d 186, 198 (2001); Williamson v. U.S., 512 U.S. 594, 600 (1994); but see Chandler v. Com., 249 Va. 270, 279, 455 S.E.2d 219, 225 (1995) ("*Williamson*, however, concerned the interpretation of the Federal Rules of Evidence, not applicable here").

Note that statements against interest made to police investigators are particularly vulnerable to constitutional, confrontation clause objections, since they are often "testimonial" under the United States Supreme Court's Confrontation Clause jurisprudence.

FED. R. EV. 804(B)(4) STATEMENT OF PERSONAL OR FAMILY HISTORY.

A statement about:

(A) the declarant's own birth, adoption, legitimacy, ancestry, marriage, divorce, relationship by blood, adoption, or marriage, or similar facts of personal or family history, even though the declarant had no way of acquiring personal knowledge about that fact; or

(B) another person concerning any of these facts, as well as death, if the declarant was related to the person by blood, adoption, or marriage or was so intimately associated with the person's family that the declarant's information is likely to be accurate.

VA. R. EV. 2:804(B)(4) STATEMENT OF PERSONAL OR FAMILY HISTORY.

If no better evidence is available, a statement made before the existence of the controversy, concerning family relationships or pedigree of a person, made by a member of the family or relative.

Comparison and Commentary

Both the Virginia and federal rules contain a hearsay exception for statements regarding family relationships and ancestry. The Virginia rule requires qualifying statements to arise before "the existence of the controversy" being litigated. Other than that, the exceptions are similar. There is little case law on their application.

VA. R. EV. 2:804(B)(5) STATEMENT BY PARTY INCAPABLE OF TESTIFYING.

Code § 8.01-397, entitled "Corroboration required and evidence receivable when one party incapable of testifying," presently provides:

In an action by or against a person who, from any cause, is

incapable of testifying, or by or against the committee, trustee, executor, administrator, heir, or other representative of the person so incapable of testifying, no judgment or decree shall be rendered in favor of an adverse or interested party founded on his uncorroborated testimony. In any such action, whether such adverse party testifies or not, all entries, memoranda, and declarations by the party so incapable of testifying made while he was capable, relevant to the matter in issue, may be received as evidence in all proceedings including without limitation those to which a person under a disability is a party. The phrase "from any cause" as used in this section shall not include situations in which the party who is incapable of testifying has rendered himself unable to testify by an intentional self-inflicted injury.

For the purposes of this section, and in addition to corroboration by any other competent evidence, an entry authored by an adverse or interested party contained in a business record may be competent evidence for corroboration of the testimony of an adverse or interested party. If authentication of the business record is not admitted in a request for admission, such business record shall be authenticated by a person other than the author of the entry who is not an adverse or interested party whose conduct is at issue in the allegations of the complaint.

Comparison and Commentary

Rule 804(b)(5) contains Virginia's "dead man's statute." The federal rules do not contain a Rule 804(b)(5) and contain no analogue to this provision. The Advisory Committee note to Federal Rule of Evidence 601 recognizes the existence of such state provisions "in variety too great to convey conviction of their wisdom and effectiveness."

FED. R. EV. 804(B)(6) STATEMENT OFFERED AGAINST A PARTY THAT WRONGFULLY CAUSED THE DECLARANT'S UNAVAILABILITY. A statement offered against a party that wrongfully caused--or acquiesced in wrongfully causing--the declarant's unavailability as a witness, and did so intending that result.

Comparison and Commentary

The federal evidence rules include a "forfeiture by wrongdoing" exception to the hearsay prohibition. Virginia's codified rules of evidence and case law do not contain this exception. Virginia cases have recently applied the parallel federal confrontation clause "forfeiture by wrongdoing" exception. See, e.g., Crawford v. Com., 281 Va. 84, 111, 704 S.E.2d 107, 123 (2011) (referencing "the forfeiture by wrongdoing doctrine, as it was defined in Giles [v. California, 554 U.S. 353 (2008)]"). Explicit reference to the federal forfeiture exception to the Sixth Amendment confrontation requirement without acknowledging the existence (or not) of an underlying state forfeiture hearsay exception leaves a gap in Virginia evidence law. Hearsay is generally prohibited in Virginia, see Rule 2:802; therefore "testimonial hearsay" as was at issue in the *Crawford v. Com.* case, referenced above, must satisfy the defendant's confrontation right *and* fall within a hearsay exception to be admissible. The Virginia case law conflating the two inquiries – see, e.g., Crawford v. Com., 53 Va. App. 138, 148, 670 S.E.2d 15, 20 (2008) superseded on reh'g en banc, 55 Va. App. 457, 686 S.E.2d 557 (2009) ("The trial court ruled the affidavit was testimonial but was admissible under the forfeiture-by-wrongdoing exception to the hearsay rule, as explained by the Commonwealth, and, thus, that its admission did not violate appellant's confrontation rights.") – will eventually need to be untangled.

FED. R. EV. 805. HEARSAY WITHIN HEARSAY

Hearsay within hearsay is not excluded by the rule against hearsay if each part of the combined statements conforms with an exception to the rule.

VA. R. EV. 2:805. HEARSAY WITHIN HEARSAY

Hearsay included within hearsay is not excluded under the hearsay rule if each part of the combined statements conforms with an exception to the hearsay rule.

Comparison and Commentary

Both the federal and Virginia rules permit the admission of hearsay within hearsay so long as each level of hearsay is admissible under the rules. The rules are identical, with Virginia tracking the language of the federal rule prior to the 2011 restyling project.

FED. R. EV. 806. ATTACKING AND SUPPORTING THE DECLARANT'S CREDIBILITY

When a hearsay statement--or a statement described in Rule 801(d)(2)(C), (D), or (E)--has been admitted in evidence, the declarant's credibility may be attacked, and then supported, by any evidence that would be admissible for those purposes if the declarant had testified as a witness. The court may admit evidence of the declarant's inconsistent statement or conduct, regardless of when it occurred or whether the declarant had an opportunity to explain or deny it. If the party against whom the statement was admitted calls the declarant as a witness, the party may examine the declarant on the statement as if on cross-examination.

VA. R. EV. 2:806. ATTACKING AND SUPPORTING CREDIBILITY OF HEARSAY DECLARANT

When a hearsay statement has been admitted in evidence, the credibility of the declarant may be attacked, and if attacked may be supported, by any evidence which would be admissible for those purposes if the declarant had testified as a witness.

Comparison and Commentary

Both the Virginia and federal rules permit the party against whom hearsay is admitted to attack the credibility of the declarant as if the declarant had testified as a witness. The federal rule includes a clarification, unnecessary in the Virginia rule, that this allowance extends to statements admitted as "not hearsay" under certain provisions of Rule 801. The federal rule also clarifies that the requirements of Rule 613 do not apply in this context and that a party may call the declarant as a witness and then proceed as if on cross-examination. Virginia's rule (and case law) does not address this scenario.

FED. R. EV. 807. RESIDUAL EXCEPTION

(a) In General. Under the following circumstances, a hearsay statement is not excluded by the rule against hearsay even if the statement is not specifically covered by a hearsay exception in Rule 803 or 804:

(1) the statement has equivalent circumstantial guarantees of trustworthiness;

(2) it is offered as evidence of a material fact;

(3) it is more probative on the point for which it is offered than any other evidence that the proponent can obtain through reasonable efforts; and

(4) admitting it will best serve the purposes of these rules and the interests of justice.

(b) Notice. The statement is admissible only if, before the trial or hearing, the proponent gives an adverse party reasonable notice of the intent to offer the statement and its particulars, including the declarant's name and address, so that the party has a fair opportunity to meet it.

Comparison and Commentary

There is no residual exception, i.e., Rule 2:807, in the Virginia rules and no formal analogue to the federal "residual" or catch-all hearsay exception. See Codification Commentary to Rule 2:804 (noting that the residual exception common to other jurisdictions "has not been recognized in Virginia, and is not included in the Virginia Rules of Evidence"). Nevertheless, the Virginia courts have been open to crafting novel hearsay exceptions when the need arises. See Robinson v. Com., 258 Va. 3, 10, 516 S.E.2d 475, 479 (1999) (acknowledging that no hearsay exception applied to allow a price tag to be relied on as proof of the price of an item, but determining that "the common-sense approach to the problem is to recognize an exception to the hearsay rule in shoplifting cases permitting the admission into evidence of price tags regularly affixed to items of personality offered for sale or, in substitution, testimony concerning the amounts shown on such tags when, as in this case, there is no objection to such testimony on best evidence grounds"); Hanson v. Com., 14 Va. App. 173, 185, 416 S.E.2d 14, 21 (1992) (relying on case law from other jurisdictions applying residual exceptions, to create an exception for a postmark "without an agent to verify how such marks are affixed in the normal course of business by the postal service"). The exception recognized in *Robinson* is now codified as Rule 2:803(24).

Other miscellaneous hearsay exceptions can be found in Virginia statutes permitting affidavits swearing to: motor vehicle damage, Va.

Code § 8.01-416; non-residence, § 8.01-414; and publication, § 8.01-415. Motor vehicle value can be established through certain trade publications, § 8.01-419.1, and life expectancy through a statutory table, § 8.01-419.

ARTICLE IX. AUTHENTICATION

FED. R. EV. 901. AUTHENTICATING OR IDENTIFYING EVIDENCE

(a) In General. To satisfy the requirement of authenticating or identifying an item of evidence, the proponent must produce evidence sufficient to support a finding that the item is what the proponent claims it is.

(b) Examples. The following are examples only--not a complete list--of evidence that satisfies the requirement:

(1) Testimony of a Witness with Knowledge. Testimony that an item is what it is claimed to be.

(2) Nonexpert Opinion About Handwriting. A nonexpert's opinion that handwriting is genuine, based on a familiarity with it that was not acquired for the current litigation.

(3) Comparison by an Expert Witness or the Trier of Fact. A comparison with an authenticated specimen by an expert witness or the trier of fact.

(4) Distinctive Characteristics and the Like. The appearance, contents, substance, internal patterns, or other distinctive characteristics of the item, taken together with all the circumstances.

(5) Opinion About a Voice. An opinion identifying a person's voice--whether heard firsthand or through mechanical or electronic transmission or recording--based on hearing the voice at any time under circumstances that connect it with the alleged speaker.

(6) Evidence About a Telephone Conversation. For a telephone conversation, evidence that a call was made to the number assigned at the time to:

> **(A)** a particular person, if circumstances, including self-identification, show that the person answering was the one called; or

> **(B)** a particular business, if the call was made to a business and the call related to business reasonably transacted over the telephone.

(7) Evidence About Public Records. Evidence that:

> **(A)** a document was recorded or filed in a public office as authorized by law; or

> **(B)** a purported public record or statement is from the office where items of this kind are kept.

(8) Evidence About Ancient Documents or Data Compilations. For a document or data compilation, evidence that it:

> **(A)** is in a condition that creates no suspicion about its authenticity;

> **(B)** was in a place where, if authentic, it would likely be; and

> **(C)** is at least 20 years old when offered.

(9) Evidence About a Process or System. Evidence describing a process or system and showing that it produces an accurate result.

(10) Methods Provided by a Statute or Rule. Any method of authentication or identification allowed by a federal statute or a rule prescribed by the Supreme Court.

VA. R. EV. 2:901. REQUIREMENT OF AUTHENTICATION OR IDENTIFICATION

The requirement of authentication or identification as a condition precedent to admissibility is satisfied by evidence sufficient to support a finding that the thing in question is what its proponent claims.

Comparison and Commentary

The Virginia and federal rules contain identical authentication standards, expressed in Federal Rule 901(a) and Rule 2:901. Minor textual distinctions arise from Virginia's mirroring of the language of the federal rule prior to the style revision and the substitution of the word "thing" for "matter." No substantive difference is reflected in these distinctions. The authentication standard "is not particularly strict"; "'Authentication is merely the process of showing that a document is genuine and that it is what its proponent claims it to be.'" Jackson v. Com., 13 Va. App. 599, 602, 413 S.E.2d 662, 664 (1992).

The main difference between the respective rules is that the federal rule provides a list of examples of evidence that can satisfy the authentication requirement. The federal examples are illustrative only, however, and the federal illustrations are consistent with Virginia case law on authentication. Authentication is, after all, a species of relevance and the federal and Virginia rules take an identical approach to defining relevance and conditional relevance. See Comparison and Commentary for Rules 104(b) and 401.

In Virginia, as in the federal system, the proponent of fungible evidence like drugs, "must establish only the vital links in the chain of custody"; "[o]ther gaps in the chain go to the weight of the evidence rather than its admissibility." Branham v. Com., 283 Va. 273, 282, 720 S.E.2d 74, 79 (2012); United States v. Scott, 19 F.3d 1238, 1245 (7th Cir. 1994) ("the government does not need to prove a 'perfect' chain of custody, and any gaps in the chain "go to the weight of the evidence and not its admissibility"). In addition to establishing that an item is what the proponent purports it to be, the proponent must "'show with reasonable certainty that there has been no alteration or substitution of the item.'" *Branham* at 282.

FED. R. EV. 902. EVIDENCE THAT IS SELF-AUTHENTICATING

The following items of evidence are self-authenticating; they require no extrinsic evidence of authenticity in order to be admitted:

(1) Domestic Public Documents That Are Sealed and Signed. A document that bears:

> (A) a seal purporting to be that of the United States; any state, district, commonwealth, territory, or insular possession of the United States; the former Panama Canal Zone; the Trust Territory of the Pacific Islands; a political subdivision of any of these entities; or a department, agency, or officer of any entity named above; and

> (B) a signature purporting to be an execution or attestation.

(2) Domestic Public Documents That Are Not Sealed but Are Signed and Certified. A document that bears no seal if:

> (A) it bears the signature of an officer or employee of an entity named in Rule 902(1)(A); and

> (B) another public officer who has a seal and official duties within that same entity certifies under seal--or its equivalent--that the signer has the official capacity and that the signature is genuine.

(3) Foreign Public Documents. A document that purports to be signed or attested by a person who is authorized by a foreign country's law to do so. The document must be accompanied by a final certification that certifies the genuineness of the signature and official position of the signer or attester--or of any foreign official whose certificate of genuineness relates to the signature or attestation or is in a chain of certificates of genuineness relating to the signature or attestation. The certification may be made by a secretary of a United States embassy or legation; by a consul general, vice consul, or consular agent of the United States; or by a diplomatic or consular official of the foreign country assigned or accredited to the United States. If all parties have been given a reasonable opportunity to investigate the document's authenticity and accuracy, the court may, for good cause, either:

(A) order that it be treated as presumptively authentic without final certification; or

(B) allow it to be evidenced by an attested summary with or without final certification.

(4) Certified Copies of Public Records. A copy of an official record--or a copy of a document that was recorded or filed in a public office as authorized by law--if the copy is certified as correct by:

(A) the custodian or another person authorized to make the certification; or

(B) a certificate that complies with Rule 902(1), (2), or (3), a federal statute, or a rule prescribed by the Supreme Court.

(5) Official Publications. A book, pamphlet, or other publication purporting to be issued by a public authority.

(6) Newspapers and Periodicals. Printed material purporting to

be a newspaper or periodical.

(7) Trade Inscriptions and the Like. An inscription, sign, tag, or label purporting to have been affixed in the course of business and indicating origin, ownership, or control.

(8) Acknowledged Documents. A document accompanied by a certificate of acknowledgment that is lawfully executed by a notary public or another officer who is authorized to take acknowledgments.

(9) Commercial Paper and Related Documents. Commercial paper, a signature on it, and related documents, to the extent allowed by general commercial law.

(10) Presumptions Under a Federal Statute. A signature, document, or anything else that a federal statute declares to be presumptively or prima facie genuine or authentic.

(11) Certified Domestic Records of a Regularly Conducted Activity. The original or a copy of a domestic record that meets the requirements of Rule 803(6)(A)-(C), as shown by a certification of the custodian or another qualified person that complies with a federal statute or a rule prescribed by the Supreme Court. Before the trial or hearing, the proponent must give an adverse party reasonable written notice of the intent to offer the record--and must make the record and certification available for inspection--so that the party has a fair opportunity to challenge them.

(12) Certified Foreign Records of a Regularly Conducted Activity. In a civil case, the original or a copy of a foreign record that meets the requirements of Rule 902(11), modified as follows: the certification, rather than complying with a federal statute or Supreme Court rule, must be signed in a manner that, if falsely made, would subject the maker to a criminal penalty in the country where the certification is

signed. The proponent must also meet the notice requirements of Rule 902(11).

VA. R. EV. 2:902. SELF-AUTHENTICATION (Rule 2:902(6) derived from Code § 8.01-390.3 and Code § 8.01-391(D))

Additional proof of authenticity as a condition precedent to admissibility is not required with respect to the following:

(1) Domestic Public Records Offered in Compliance With Statute. Public records authenticated or certified as provided under a statute of the Commonwealth.

(2) Foreign Public Documents. A document purporting to be executed or attested in his official capacity by a person authorized by the laws of a foreign country to make the execution or attestation, and accompanied by a final certification as to the genuineness of the signature and official position (a) of the executing or attesting person, or (b) of any foreign official whose certificate of genuineness of signature and official position relates to the execution or attestation or is in a chain of certification of genuineness of signature and official position relating to the execution or attestation. A final certification may be made by a secretary of embassy or legation, consul general, consul, vice consul, or consular agent of the United States, or a diplomatic or consular official of the foreign country assigned or accredited to the United States. If reasonable opportunity has been given to all parties to investigate the authenticity and accuracy of official documents, the court may for good cause shown order that they be treated as presumptively authentic without final certification or permit them to be evidenced by an attested summary with or without final certification.

(3) Presumptions Created by Law. Any signature, document, or other matter declared by any law of the United States or of this Commonwealth, to be presumptively or prima facie genuine or authentic.

(4) Medical Records and Medical Bills in Particular Actions. Where authorized by statute, medical records and medical bills, offered upon the forms of authentication specified in the Code of Virginia.

(5) Specific Certificates of Analysis and Reports. Certificates of analysis and official reports prepared by designated persons or facilities, when authenticated in accordance with applicable statute.

(6) Certified Records of a Regularly Conducted Activity.

(a) In any civil proceeding where a business record is material and otherwise admissible, authentication of the record and the foundation required by subdivision (6) of Rule 2:803 may be laid by (i) witness testimony, (ii) a certification of the authenticity of and foundation for the record made by the custodian of such record or other qualified witness either by affidavit or by declaration pursuant to Code § 8.01-4.3, or (iii) a combination of witness testimony and a certification.

(b) The proponent of a business record shall (i) give written notice to all other parties if a certification under this section will be relied upon in whole or in part in authenticating and laying the foundation for admission of such record and (ii) provide a copy of the record and the certification to all other parties, so that all parties have a fair opportunity to challenge the record and certification. The notice and copy of the record and certification shall be provided no later than 15 days in advance of the trial or hearing, unless an order of the court specifies a different time. Objections shall be made within five days thereafter, unless an order of the court specifies a different time. If any party timely objects to reliance upon the certification, the authentication and foundation required by subdivision (6) of Rule 2:803 shall be made by witness testimony unless the objection is withdrawn.

(c) A certified business record that satisfies the requirements of this section shall be self-authenticating and requires no extrinsic evidence of authenticity.

(d) A copy of a business record may be offered in lieu of an original upon satisfaction of the requirements of Code § 8.01-391(D) by witness testimony, a certification, or a combination of testimony and a certification.

Comparison and Commentary

The federal and Virginia rules recognize the self-authentication of certain categories of evidence. The key distinction is that the federal rule itself sets out the criteria for self-authentication, while the Virginia rule largely relies on the vast laundry list of authentication statutes in the Virginia Code (see below).

The two categories that the Virginia rule addresses internally are foreign public documents, 2:902(2), and business records, 2:902(6). Foreign public records are treated the same as in the federal rule, with the Virginia rule drafters adopting, without alteration, the language of unrestyled Rule 902(3). The business records provision, Rule 2:902(6), tracks Va. Code § 8.01-390.3. The code provision, applicable only to civil cases, creates a mechanism by which a proponent of a business record can authenticate the record without relying on live witness testimony of the record's custodian. The provision is similar to Federal Rule 902(11), although the federal rule contemplates admission even over objection, while the Virginia version states that a timely objection triggers a requirement that authentication be established through live testimony.

The Virginia Rule's other provisions: 2:902(1) (domestic public records), 2:902(3) (presumptions created by law), 2:902(4) (medical records) and 2:902(5) (specific certificates of analysis and reports) all state that where some other legal provision establishes the authenticity of a document, that document is self-authenticating under the evidence code. Rule 2:902 does not, however, cross-reference the applicable provisions which are scattered throughout the Virginia Code.

For examples of statutes relating to 2:902(1), domestic public records, see Va. Code § 8.01-389 (judicial records); § 8.01-390 (non-judicial, official records); § 8.01-390.1 (educational records); § 8.01-390.2 (medical examiner reports); § 32.1-272 (vital records); § 46.2-215 (records of Department of Motor Vehicles); Hall v. Com., 15 Va. App. 170, 175, 421 S.E.2d 887, 890 (1992) (discussing authentication of Virginia DMV records).

Virginia Rule 2:902(3) is similar to Federal Rule 902(10), deeming self-authenticating any record established by Virginia or federal law to be presumptively authentic. The federal version references only federal law. This Virginia provision might allow state litigants to cross-reference the federal rule for examples of self-authentication as Federal Rule 902 is itself "federal law" and deems numerous items not captured in the Virginia rule to be self-authenticating (e.g., newspapers).

For examples of statutes relating to 2:902(4), medical records, see Va. Code § 8.01-413.01 (medical bills); § 16.1-88.2 (records of treatment and bills) and § 16.1-235.1 (medical records in juvenile or domestic relations district court).

For examples of statutes relating to 2:902(5), certificates of analysis, see Va. Code § 18.2-268.7 (blood tests for drugs alcohol content), § 18.2-268.9 (breath-tests), § 19.2-188.1 (forensic and drug analysis).

Fed. R. Ev. 903. Subscribing Witness's Testimony

A subscribing witness's testimony is necessary to authenticate a writing only if required by the law of the jurisdiction that governs its validity.

Va. R. Ev. 2:903. SUBSCRIBING WITNESS TESTIMONY NOT NECESSARY

The testimony of a subscribing witness is not necessary to authenticate a writing unless required by the laws of the jurisdiction whose laws govern the validity of the writing.

Comparison and Commentary

The federal and Virginia rules both similarly dispense with the requirement that the person who filled out or signed a document testify in order to authenticate the document. Rather, the document can be authenticated by alternate means.

ARTICLE X. BEST EVIDENCE

FED. R. EV. 1001. DEFINITIONS THAT APPLY TO THIS ARTICLE

In this article:

(a) A "writing" consists of letters, words, numbers, or their equivalent set down in any form.

(b) A "recording" consists of letters, words, numbers, or their equivalent recorded in any manner.

(c) A "photograph" means a photographic image or its equivalent stored in any form.

(d) An "original" of a writing or recording means the writing or recording itself or any counterpart intended to have the same effect by the person who executed or issued it. For electronically stored information, "original" means any printout--or other output readable by sight--if it accurately reflects the information. An "original" of a photograph includes the negative or a print from it.

(e) A "duplicate" means a counterpart produced by a mechanical, photographic, chemical, electronic, or other equivalent process or technique that accurately reproduces the original.

VA. R. EV. 2:1001. DEFINITIONS

For purposes of this Article, the following definitions are applicable.

(1) **Writings**. "Writings" consist of letters, words, or numbers, or their equivalent, set down by handwriting, typewriting, printing, photostating, photographing, magnetic impulse,

mechanical or electronic recording, or other form of data compilation or preservation.

(2) Original. An "original" of a writing is the writing itself or any other writing intended to have the same effect by a person executing or issuing it.

Comparison and Commentary

Both the Virginia and federal rules include a "Best Evidence" rule. The rule applies when a party attempts to "prove the content" of a "writing" through the use of secondary evidence.

The key distinction between the federal and Virginia variants is that, while the federal rule defines "writing" to include all manner of recorded information (e.g., photographs, videotapes), "the best evidence rule in Virginia applies only to writings." Brown v. Com., 54 Va. App. 107, 116 & n.5, 676 S.E.2d 326, 330 & n.5 (Va. App. 2009). As a consequence, a party can introduce testimony about the contents of a video or photograph, without accounting for the original in Virginia state court, but not in federal court. Id. at 330 & n.5 (holding that rule did not apply because "a videotape is not a writing" and noting Virginia's divergence from other jurisdictions in limiting rule to writings); Midkiff v. Com., 280 Va. 216, 219, 694 S.E.2d 576, 577 (Va. 2010) (noting that "application of the rule is limited to written documents" in rejecting a challenge to recreation of computer images). Presumably Virginia courts would consider electronic communications to be "writings," see Rule 2:1001(1), although case law has not yet developed on this important point. Cobb v. Com., 1526-12-1, 2013 WL 5744363 (Va. App. 2013) (unpublished) ("We assume without deciding that a text message qualifies as a 'writing.'"); cf. Comparison and Commentary to Federal Rule 101(b)(6).

Another distinction is found in Virginia's treatment of duplicates. The divergence begins in Rule 2:1001 which, unlike the federal rule, does not contain a definition of "duplicate." But as discussed in the Comparison and Commentary to Rule 2:1003, Virginia case law endorses reliance on duplicates in a manner similar to that authorized by the federal rule.

FED. R. EV. 1002. REQUIREMENT OF THE ORIGINAL

An original writing, recording, or photograph is required in order to prove its content unless these rules or a federal statute provides otherwise.

VA. R. EV. 2:1002. REQUIREMENT OF PRODUCTION OF ORIGINAL

To prove the content of a writing, the original writing is required, except as otherwise provided in these Rules, other Rules of the Supreme Court of Virginia, or in a Virginia statute.

Comparison and Commentary

Both the federal and Virginia Best Evidence rules apply only when a party is attempting to *prove the content* of a writing. As a result, the rules do not apply when witnesses testify about matters they perceived first hand that happen to also be captured in writings. Watkins v. Com., 1558-13-1, 2014 WL 3579883 (Va. App. 2014) (unpublished) (ruling that best evidence rule was violated where prosecution "sought to prove the content of the price tags" with testimony; "it was required either to produce those price tags or to account for their unavailability. Alternatively, ..., the Commonwealth could have established that [the testifying witness] had a basis— independent of the price tags themselves—for knowing the value of the stolen jeans...."); U.S. v. Smith, 566 F.3d 410, 414 (4th Cir. 2009) ("Just because Special Agent Cheramie consulted books and computer databases in reaching his conclusion about the firearms' place of manufacture does not mean that his testimony was offered 'to prove the content' of the books and computer files."). Rather, it is only when secondary evidence, such as testimony or recreations, is offered to communicate the content of a "writing" itself that the rule applies. Seiler v. Lucasfilm, Ltd., 808 F.2d 1316, 1319 (9th Cir. 1986). As a consequence, the primary utility of understanding the Best Evidence rule is to ward off frivolous "best evidence" objections.

FED. R. EV. 1003. ADMISSIBILITY OF DUPLICATES

A duplicate is admissible to the same extent as the original unless a genuine question is raised about the original's authenticity or the circumstances make it unfair to admit the duplicate.

VA. R. EV. 2:1003. USE OF SUBSTITUTE CHECKS
(derived from Code § 8.01-391.1(A) and (B))

(a) Admissibility generally. A substitute check created pursuant to the federal Check Clearing for the 21st Century Evidence Act, 12 U.S.C. § 5001 et seq., shall be admissible in evidence in any Virginia legal proceeding, civil or criminal, to the same extent the original check would be.

(b) Presumption from designation and legend. A document received from a banking institution that is designated as a "substitute check" and that bears the legend "This is a legal copy of your check. You can use it the same way you would use the original check" shall be presumed to be a substitute check created pursuant to the Act applicable under subdivision (a) of this Rule.

Comparison and Commentary

Federal Rule 1003 allows duplicates to be used in most circumstances in place of originals. Virginia's codification of the evidence rules contains two provisions regarding duplicates, 2:1003 and 2:1005, both of which carry on at surprising length about narrow situations when duplicates are admissible. Despite this apparent difference, the same general principal permitting the use of a duplicate recognized by Federal Rule 1003 is recognized in Virginia. See Allocca v. Allocca, 23 Va. App. 571, 579, 478 S.E.2d 702, 706 (Va. App. 1996) ("if a copy can properly be treated as a 'duplicate original,' the copy is admissible without regard to the availability of the original"); cf. Myrick v. Com., 13 Va. App. 333, 339, 412 S.E.2d 176, 179 (1991).

FED. R. EV. 1004. ADMISSIBILITY OF OTHER EVIDENCE OF CONTENT

An original is not required and other evidence of the content of a writing, recording, or photograph is admissible if:

(a) all the originals are lost or destroyed, and not by the proponent acting in bad faith;

(b) an original cannot be obtained by any available judicial process;

(c) the party against whom the original would be offered had control of the original; was at that time put on notice, by pleadings or otherwise, that the original would be a subject of proof at the trial or hearing; and fails to produce it at the trial or hearing; or

(d) the writing, recording, or photograph is not closely related to a controlling issue.

VA. R. EV. 2:1004. ADMISSIBILITY OF OTHER EVIDENCE OF CONTENTS

The original is not required, and other evidence of the contents of a writing is admissible if:

(a) Originals lost or destroyed. All originals are lost or have been destroyed, unless the proponent lost or destroyed them in bad faith; or

(b) Original not obtainable. No original can be obtained by any available judicial process or procedure, unless the proponent acted in bad faith to render the original unavailable; or

(c) Original in possession of opponent. At a time when an original was under the control of the party against whom offered, that party was put on notice, by the pleadings or otherwise, that the contents would be a subject of proof at the hearing, and that party does not produce the original at the hearing; or

(d) Collateral matters. The writing is not closely related to a controlling issue.

Comparison and Commentary

Both the federal and Virginia rules permit the use of secondary evidence when the original has been lost, is otherwise unattainable, or destroyed (and not in bad faith by its proponent) or the evidence is not significant. This provision takes much of the sting out of the Best Evidence rule.

FED. R. EV. 1005. COPIES OF PUBLIC RECORDS TO PROVE CONTENT

The proponent may use a copy to prove the content of an official record--or of a document that was recorded or filed in a public office as authorized by law--if these conditions are met: the record or document is otherwise admissible; and the copy is certified as correct in accordance with Rule 902(4) or is testified to be correct by a witness who has compared it with the original. If no such copy can be obtained by reasonable diligence, then the proponent may use other evidence to prove the content.

VA. R. EV. 2:1005. ADMISSIBILITY OF COPIES (derived from Code § 8.01-391)

In addition to admissibility of copies of documents as provided in Rules 2:1002 and 2:1004, and by statute, copies may be used in lieu of original documents as follows:

(a) Whenever the original of any official publication or other record has been filed in an action or introduced as evidence, the court may order the original to be returned to its custodian, retaining in its stead a copy thereof. The court may make any order to prevent the improper use of the original.

(b) If any department, division, institution, agency, board, or commission of this Commonwealth, of another state or country, or of the United States, or of any political subdivision or agency of the same, acting pursuant to the law of the respective jurisdiction or other proper authority, has copied any record made in the performance of its official duties, such copy shall be as admissible into evidence as the original, whether the original is in existence or not, provided that such copy is authenticated as a true copy either by the custodian of said record or by the person to whom said custodian reports, if they are different, and is accompanied by a certificate that such person does in fact have the custody.

(c) If any court or clerk's office of a court of this Commonwealth, of another state or country, or of the United States, or of any political subdivision or agency of the same, has copied any record made in the performance of its official duties, such copy shall be admissible into evidence as the original, whether the original is in existence or not, provided that such copy is authenticated as a true copy by a clerk or deputy clerk of such court.

(d) If any business or member of a profession or calling in the regular course of business or activity has made any record or received or transmitted any document, and again in the regular course of business has caused any or all of such record or document to be copied, the copy shall be as admissible in evidence as the original, whether the original exists or not, provided that such copy is satisfactorily identified and authenticated as a true copy by a custodian of such record or by the person to whom said custodian reports, if they be different, and is accompanied by a certificate that said person does in fact have the custody. Copies in the regular course of business shall be deemed to include reproduction at a later time, if done in good faith and without intent to defraud. Copies in the regular course of business shall include items such as checks which are regularly copied before transmission to another person or bank, or records which are acted upon without receipt of the original when the original is retained by another party.

The original of which a copy has been made may be destroyed in the regular course of business unless its preservation is required by law, or its validity has been questioned.

(e) The introduction in an action of a copy under this Rule neither precludes the introduction or admission of the original nor the introduction of a copy or the original in another action.

(f) Copy, as used in these Rules, shall include photographs, microphotographs, photostats, microfilm, microcard, printouts or other reproductions of electronically stored data, or copies from optical disks, electronically transmitted facsimiles, or any other reproduction of an original from a process which forms a durable medium for its recording, storing, and reproducing.

Comparison and Commentary

The federal and Virginia rules permit copies of certain official records in lieu of an original to prove their content. Virginia's rule also extends to copies of business records. As noted in the Comparison and Commentary to Rule 2:1003, the absence of a generic duplicates provision in Virginia's evidence rules, alongside specific duplicates provisions like 2:1003 and 2:1005 may be misleading. Virginia case law suggests that duplicates can be admitted outside of the narrow circumstances (business and official records) set forth in the evidence code. Compare Allocca v. Allocca, 23 Va.App. 571, 579, 478 S.E.2d 702, 706 (Va. App. 1996) (rejecting best evidence challenge to a divorce agreement where there was no allegation that the duplicate introduced into evidence was untrustworthy) with Fed. R. Ev. 1003 (allowing duplicate "unless a genuine question is raised about the original's authenticity").

FED. R. EV. 1006. SUMMARIES TO PROVE CONTENT

The proponent may use a summary, chart, or calculation to prove the content of voluminous writings, recordings, or photographs that cannot be conveniently examined in court. The proponent must make the originals or duplicates available for examination or copying, or both, by other parties at a reasonable time and place. And the court may order the proponent to produce them in court.

VA. R. EV. 2:1006. SUMMARIES

The contents of voluminous writings that, although admissible, cannot conveniently be examined in court may be represented in the form of a chart, summary, or calculation. Reasonably in advance of the offer of such chart, summary, or calculation, the originals or duplicates shall be made available for examination or copying, or both, by other parties at a reasonable time and place. The court may order that they be produced in court.

Comparison and Commentary

Both the federal and Virginia rules permit the use of summaries of voluminous writings when circumstances warrant.

FED. R. EV. 1007. TESTIMONY OR STATEMENT OF A PARTY TO PROVE CONTENT

The proponent may prove the content of a writing, recording, or photograph by the testimony, deposition, or written statement of the party against whom the evidence is offered. The proponent need not account for the original.

VA. R. EV. 2:1007. TESTIMONY OR WRITTEN ADMISSION OF A PARTY

Contents of writings may be proved by the admission of the party against whom offered without accounting for the nonproduction of the original.

Comparison and Commentary

Both the federal and Virginia rules carve out an exception to the Best Evidence rule that allows a party to use statements of an opposing party in place of an original.

FED. R. EV. 1008. FUNCTIONS OF THE COURT AND JURY

Ordinarily, the court determines whether the proponent has fulfilled the factual conditions for admitting other evidence of the content of a writing, recording, or photograph under Rule 1004 or 1005. But in a jury trial, the jury determines--in accordance with Rule 104(b)--any issue about whether:

(a) an asserted writing, recording, or photograph ever existed;

(b) another one produced at the trial or hearing is the original; or

(c) other evidence of content accurately reflects the content.

Va. R. Ev. 2:1008. Functions Of Court And Jury

Whenever the admissibility of other evidence of contents or writings under these provisions depends upon the fulfillment of a condition of fact, the question whether the condition has been fulfilled is ordinarily for the court to determine. However, when an issue is raised whether (1) the asserted writing ever existed, or (2) another writing produced at the trial is the original, or (3) other evidence of contents correctly reflects the contents, the issue is for the trier of fact to determine.

Comparison and Commentary

Both the federal and Virginia rules similarly apportion the responsibilities of judge and jury in assessing the applicability of the Best Evidence rule.

ARTICLE XI. MISCELLANEOUS RULES

FED. R. EV. 1101. APPLICABILITY OF THE RULES

(a) To Courts and Judges. These rules apply to proceedings before:

- United States district courts;

- United States bankruptcy and magistrate judges;

- United States courts of appeals;

- the United States Court of Federal Claims; and

- the district courts of Guam, the Virgin Islands, and the Northern Mariana Islands.

(b) To Cases and Proceedings. These rules apply in:

- civil cases and proceedings, including bankruptcy, admiralty, and maritime cases;

- criminal cases and proceedings; and

- contempt proceedings, except those in which the court may act summarily.

(c) Rules on Privilege. The rules on privilege apply to all stages of a case or proceeding.

(d) Exceptions. These rules--except for those on privilege--do not apply to the following:

(1) the court's determination, under Rule 104(a), on a preliminary question of fact governing admissibility;

(2) grand-jury proceedings; and

(3) miscellaneous proceedings such as:

- extradition or rendition;

- issuing an arrest warrant, criminal summons, or search warrant;

- a preliminary examination in a criminal case;

- sentencing;

- granting or revoking probation or supervised release; and

- considering whether to release on bail or otherwise.

(e) Other Statutes and Rules. A federal statute or a rule prescribed by the Supreme Court may provide for admitting or excluding evidence independently from these rules.

VA. R. EV. 2:1101. APPLICABILITY OF EVIDENTIARY RULES

(a) Proceedings to which applicable generally. Evidentiary rules apply generally to (1) all civil actions and (2) proceedings in a criminal case (including preliminary hearings in criminal cases), and to contempt proceedings (except contempt proceedings in which the court may act summarily), in the Supreme Court of Virginia, the Court of Appeals of Virginia, the State Corporation Commission (when acting as a court of record), the circuit courts, the general district courts (except when acting as a small claims court as provided by statute), and the juvenile and domestic relations district courts.

(b) Law of privilege. The law with respect to privileges applies at all stages of all actions, cases, and proceedings.

(c) Permissive application. Except as otherwise provided by statute or rule, adherence to the Rules of Evidence (other than with respect to privileges) is permissive, not mandatory, in the following situations:

> (1) Criminal proceedings other than (i) trial, (ii) preliminary hearings, (iii) sentencing proceedings before a jury, and (iv) capital murder sentencing hearings.

> (2) Administrative proceedings.

Comparison and Commentary

The Virginia and federal rules both enumerate the proceedings to which they do and do not apply. The respective jurisdictions have different institutional components so the lists diverge, but the guiding principle is similar for each. More formal, trial-like proceedings are governed by the rules of evidence; informal proceedings (e.g., grand jury, sentencing, summary contempt) are not. One major difference between the respective rules concerns preliminary examinations in criminal cases. The federal rule excludes "a preliminary examination" in a criminal case from the coverage of the evidence rules; the Virginia rule includes "preliminary hearings in criminal cases" within the rules' coverage. This provision comes from a separate Virginia Code section. See Va. Code §19.2-183(B) (requiring preliminary hearing judge to "hear testimony presented for and against the accused in accordance with the rules of evidence applicable to criminal trials in this Commonwealth").

Virginia's rule states that its evidence rules apply to sentencing proceedings before a jury and capital murder sentencing hearings. The former do not exist in federal court. Federal capital sentencing hearings are not governed by the rules of evidence. 18 U.S.C.A. § 3593(c) ("Information is admissible regardless of its admissibility under the rules governing admission of evidence at criminal trials except that information may be excluded if its probative value is outweighed by the danger of creating unfair prejudice, confusing the issues, or misleading the jury.")

Federal Rule 1101(d)(1) explicitly frees judges from the strictures of the rules of evidence when conducting preliminary determinations of admissibility under Rule 104(a). Virginia does not include this provision in the text of its rules, but the principle can be found in the commentary to the codification of Rule 2:104: "In determining admissibility, the judge is not bound by strict rules of evidence, other than privilege." Codification Commentary to Rule 2:104(a).

Both rules contain an essentially identical provision emphasizing that privilege applies at all stages of a proceeding.

FED. R. EV. 1102. AMENDMENTS

These rules may be amended as provided in 28 U.S.C. § 2072.

Comparison and Commentary

While the Virginia rules do not contain a provision discussing amendments, the Virginia Code includes specific provisions for enacting changes to the evidence rules. Va. Code § 8.01-3(E), (F). In addition, the Virginia Supreme Court has the power to promulgate its own rules. Virginia Const. Article VI § 5.

FED. R. EV. 1103. TITLE

These rules may be cited as the Federal Rules of Evidence.

Comparison and Commentary

The Virginia rules' title provision is contained in Rule 2:101.

---

please send comments and suggestions to
jbellin@wm.edu

Made in the USA
Middletown, DE
08 May 2024

54056909R00126